THE
GREAT
FRAUD
ON THE
BANK
OF
ENGLAND

THE
GREAT
FRAUD
ON THE
BANK
OF
ENGLAND

DAVID C. HANRAHAN

ROBERT HALE · LONDON

© David C. Hanrahan 2014
First published in Great Britain 2014

ISBN 978-0-7090-9595-8

Robert Hale Limited
Clerkenwell House
Clerkenwell Green
London EC1R 0HT

www.halebooks.com

A catalogue record for this book is available
from the British Library

2 4 6 8 10 9 7 5 3 1

Typeset by e-type, Liverpool
Printed in Great Britain by Berforts Information Press Ltd

Contents

Acknowledgements

This book, as usual, would not have been possible to create without the help of a great many others. My thanks and appreciation go to the following: The Hardiman Library at the National University of Ireland, Galway; I thank, in particular, Inter-Library Loans for their great efforts to get access to the Pinkerton case files for me. I am also very grateful to Yale University for the loan of the microfilm version of those files. I would like to thank Mark Vivian at Mary Evans Picture Library for his assistance. I want to thank my friends and colleagues at the School of Education, National University of Ireland, Galway; in particular, Dr Tony Hall for his friendship, regard for intellectualism and positive encouragement. I am grateful to all at Robert Hale Publishing for their professionalism, especially Alexander Stilwell and Nikki Edwards; Robert Dudley, my agent, has been invaluable as always. A special word of thanks and love goes, as usual, to my family: Margaret, for her financial expertise which was especially helpful on this book; Aisling and Michael for their encouragement, patience and computer skills; my brothers and their families. I write this book in remembrance of my mother, Mary, who was, quite simply, a great woman and mother.

CHAPTER 1

Mr Frederick Albert Warren

———•◦•———

On 4 May 1872, the well-respected and long-established Savile Row tailor, Mr Edward Hamilton Green, walked into his local branch of the Bank of England. It was the branch located at Burlington Gardens, London, often referred to as the West End or Western branch, where he had been a customer for many years. Mr Green was the proprietor of a shop at 35 Savile Row, which enjoyed a well-earned reputation as a tailors and army clothiers. The firm was run by himself and his son, Mr Edward E. Green. On this particular day, however, the elder Mr Green was accompanied by a striking young man unknown to the staff at the Bank of England. Mr Robert Fenwick, the assistant manager, came forward and was introduced by the tailor to Mr Frederick Albert Warren, a businessman from America. Mr Fenwick surveyed the obviously prosperous American as the tailor was informing him that his friend, who was over in England for business reasons, wished to open an account.

In reality, Mr Edward Hamilton Green had not known the young American all that long. He had first met Mr Warren some weeks earlier, on 18 April, when the gentleman had visited his shop with his American friend, Mr Swift, and a third man who the elder Mr Green later thought was called Mr Siebert. The son, Mr Edward E. Green, had also been present at the time.[1] It soon became clear that Mr Warren was a man who appreciated fine clothes such as those created on Savile Row and could become, the Greens realized, a potentially lucrative new customer. This realization was confirmed when both Mr Warren and Mr Swift placed considerable orders that first day. They signed the Greens' address book, using the same Enfield Road address. Many visits followed – more than twenty in fact – and multiple purchases.

Earlier on the day of their visit to the Bank of England, Mr Warren and Mr Swift had arrived at the Greens' shop, with great ceremony, in a cab loaded down with luggage. They were there for a pre-booked fitting session, but Mr Warren informed the elder Mr Green that they were in a hurry. They were on their way to Ireland, he said, having been invited there by some relatives. As Mr Green proceeded with his work of measuring, Mr Warren mentioned that he had a little problem, an inconvenience: he had in his possession, he said, an amount of money that he did not think safe to leave at his lodgings while he was away. As an American not long in the country, he did not possess a bank account in England and he needed somewhere to leave the money while he was gone.

'Is it of any amount?' the elder Mr Green asked, eager to help.

'Yes, it is some amount,' replied Mr Warren.

When Mr Green heard that the amount in question was £1,200, he was not keen to take responsibility for that much.

'I should recommend you to deposit it with some bank,' he suggested instead. Then he went further: 'My banker is close at hand.'

'We have very little time to spare,' said Mr Warren. 'We are in a hurry to get a train.'

'It will not take you long,' Mr Green reassured him. ' I can take you down there.'[2]

Hence, Mr Green led Mr Warren the short distance to the branch of the Bank of England at Burlington Gardens, where he introduced him as an American customer of his who needed to deposit some money. Mr Fenwick had assumed responsibility for assisting them because Mr Pimm, the branch manager, was absent at the time. Mr Fenwick set about arranging things as quickly as he could for someone who was obviously in a hurry and, quite clearly, a very good customer of the Greens. This was a time when the Bank of England was not just a central bank concerned with important financial matters of state, but was also engaged in conventional banking practices, having local branches and accepting deposits from the general public. Mr Warren was facilitated in opening his new Bank of England account with the minimum of fuss.

Mr Fenwick filled out the bank signature book for him. When he asked his new customer how his profession should be described, Mr Warren seemed unsure and a little hesitant. His role could be described, he explained with some circumspection, 'as an agent for others'.[3]

'Then I shall describe you as a commission agent?' suggested Mr Fenwick.

'Yes,' agreed Warren.[4]

Warren was in England, he told Mr Fenwick, because he was involved with the exciting business idea of manufacturing railway sleeping cars for use in Europe, just like those used in America. Mr Fenwick was undoubtedly impressed by the young entrepreneur who was planning to have his sleeping cars in service on the line between Paris and Vienna for the upcoming exhibition in Vienna, so that visitors from England and elsewhere would get the opportunity to try them out. He had other railway products in planning as well, such as his new design for a steam brake and a light for the front of train engines. He was clearly a man on the way up – or, at least, that was Mr Fenwick's impression of him:

> He said he had offers from three manufacturers in Birmingham ... and hoped to be in full working order before the 1st of July.[5]

Mr Fenwick asked him to sign the signature book in full, which he did as 'Frederick Albert Warren' with an address at the Golden Cross Hotel, Charing Cross. Mr Warren then deposited his £1,200, made up of a bank draft to the value of £197, bank notes worth £1,000 and £3 in coins.[6] He said that he would have more money to deposit soon and asked whether he should do so through Mr Green. Fenwick told him that was unnecessary in the future as he was now an account holder with the bank himself. He then issued him with a cheque book and told him that he could call another day to collect his 'pass book'. After that day Mr Fenwick saw Mr Warren at the bank a number of times, engaged in business.

On 1 June 1872, Colonel Peregrine Madgwick Francis was appointed as the new manager of the Bank of England branch at Burlington Gardens, taking over the position from Mr Pimm. Colonel Francis began working there on 3 June. He went away on holiday from 27 July to 28 August so only met Mr Warren for the first time on 3 September 1872. Colonel Francis was a senior bank official with thirteen years' experience behind him. Before being appointed to this position at Burlington Gardens, he had been sub-manager of the branch at Leeds and manager at Hull.[7]

By the time Colonel Francis met him, Mr Warren was an established account holder at the branch. The two men were introduced by Mr Fenwick. On that occasion Mr Warren asked Colonel Francis to hold some Portuguese bonds for him, valued at around £8,000. He also cashed a cheque of his own to the value of £100. On the following day, 4 September 1872, Mr Warren called again and deposited another £4,000 in Portuguese bonds. He then requested that the bank sell all the bonds for him. A few days later, on 9 September, he asked Colonel Francis for an advance on the sale of those bonds. He needed £2,000, he said, and this amount was advanced to him.

The bonds were subsequently sold, the advance of £2,000 recouped by the bank and the rest credited to Mr Warren's account. In the weeks that followed the transactions continued. Colonel Francis did not deal with Mr Warren himself on every occasion that he came into the bank, but he did see him there quite often. Any time they had dealings, the two men got on very well.

As their friendship developed, Mr Warren asked Colonel Francis if he would be willing to discount bills of exchange for him. These are, essentially, legal financial documents or financial instruments, like cheques or bank drafts, that promise the bearer a certain amount of money at a predetermined date, i.e. the date of maturity. If a person wishes, they can present such a bill at a bank or broker before the date of maturity and receive an amount less than its full value. This is a practice known in the trade as discounting. The bank or the broker will then claim the full value of the bill when it matures.

Colonel Francis could see no problem with discounting such bills for Mr Warren. He did claim later to have checked the authenticity of a number of the bills of exchange that were presented by Mr Warren at the beginning, all of which he found to be perfectly genuine. For example, on 29 November 1872, Mr Warren brought in two bills of exchange for discount worth £500 each, 'accepted' by the reputable London firm of Messrs Suse and Sibeth. Colonel Francis claimed later that he made some enquiries about them and they were both confirmed to be 'first-class bills'. He agreed to discount them. Mr Warren had told Colonel Francis that 'he would have some more bills of the same character, which he would ask the Bank to discount for him'.[8] So it was that the discounting of bills of exchange in this way became a routine business practice for Mr Warren, and Colonel Francis was content about undertaking it. Colonel Francis would have to admit later that very little or, in fact, no checks were carried out on the validity of the bills after the initial period.

There is little doubt that Colonel Francis, like Mr Fenwick, was impressed by the ambitious Mr Warren with his newfangled American ideas such as the railway sleeping car. Everything about him seemed most encouraging for an enthusiastic bank manager like Colonel Francis:

> ... he trusted before long to have a company formed for English purposes, which would keep a good account at the branch.[9]

Perhaps it was reasonable to accept that discounting a large number of bills of exchange to generate cash flow was necessitated by the scale of Mr Warren's new business venture. After all, Mr Warren did plan to have a number of his new sleeping cars ready for the Vienna exhibition, which was due to open on 1 May 1873, and each of the cars was estimated to cost around £4,000.[10] It is true that when Colonel Francis asked Mr Warren for some more detail regarding the design of the new steam brake he was proposing to manufacture, the American claimed that he could not reveal anything about it at that time as it had to be kept a secret. Perhaps this too sounded reasonable.

Neither did anyone think it unusual when, just before Christmas 1872, Mr Warren informed his bank that his business interests dictated that he now base himself in Birmingham quite a lot of the time. He asked Colonel Francis if, from then on, it would be permissible for him to post in most of his transactions from there, including the bills of exchange for discount. Colonel Francis had no problem with such an arrangement – whatever was most convenient for the customer. Therefore, on 30 December 1872, the first such batch of bills arrived from Birmingham along with the following letter addressed to Colonel Francis:

> Sir,
> Enclosed I hand you bills for discount as per accompanying memorandum. Will you please place the proceeds of the same to credit of my account, and oblige,
>> Yours faithfully,
>> F. A. Warren[11]

Ten bills of exchange were enclosed at a value of £4,307 4s. 6d.

CHAPTER 2

Mr Charles Johnson Horton

O n 2 December 1872, another American businessman, Mr Charles Johnson Horton, with an address at the Charing Cross Hotel, London, also opened a new bank account. The account this time was opened at the Continental Bank on Lombard Street, also known as Messrs Hartland and Co. This American client was no less impressive than the new American client of Colonel Francis at the Bank of England. Mr Horton was well dressed, rich and successful. He explained to the manager of the Continental Bank, Mr John Thomas Stanton, that he had been lucky enough to have withdrawn £7,500 of his money from Messrs Bowles Brothers before the suspension of that particular institution.[1] He deposited £1,300 in his new account and the next day called again and deposited over £235 more. After that the flow of money in and out of Mr Horton's account continued unabated.

Around the middle of January 1873, Mr Horton informed the staff at the Continental Bank that he had become so busy that he would be doing business in a different way from then on. He had decided to take on a clerk who would conduct his business dealings in London, while he would be working himself mostly from Birmingham. According to his story, Mr Horton had managed to find his new clerk, Mr Edwin Noyes, a fellow American, through an advertisement that he had seen in the *Daily Telegraph*. Mr Noyes had placed the advertisement describing himself as 'a gentleman of active business habits, and with a small capital of 300*l*.' who required 'a situation as clerk or partner',[2] and asked that inquiries be sent to him at Durrants Hotel, where he was resident at that time.

Mr Horton arrived at the hotel to meet with Edwin Noyes and was led into the coffee room, where Noyes was having his breakfast. Mr Horton had arrived in a Hansom cab and, after spending a few minutes together, the two men left in the same cab, Noyes having asked: 'Shall I go straight away with you now?'[3] In reference to all the letters that had arrived for him, Noyes told one of the waiters at Durrants Hotel, James Richardson, about his advertisement, the business proposition he was offering and the £300 security he was putting up. Richardson was not impressed and, in fact, was quite worried about Mr Noyes.

'You ought to be very careful in whose hands you place £300,' Richardson told him, no doubt taking him for a naïve foreigner.

'Oh, not with such gentlemen as these,' Noyes replied. 'I guess I'm all right.'[4]

Richardson saw him with the same man a number of other times and was aware that they had come to a business agreement. Mr Horton and Mr Noyes had a legal document drawn up by a solicitor in Cheapside, Mr David Howell. It stated that Mr Noyes would be paid an annual salary of £150 by Mr Horton for performing the duties of a clerk and manager. In the event that Mr Noyes decided to leave the position, the £300 that he had put up as security would be returned to him, without interest, providing that he had performed his duties diligently and honestly.

It was around 18 January 1873 when Mr Horton introduced Mr Edwin Noyes to Mr John Thomas Stanton and the staff at the Continental Bank. It was obvious to them that Mr Horton was very satisfied with his new business arrangement and he was quite clear in his directions to them regarding his new clerk's authority to act on his behalf:

He said Noyes was his confidential clerk, and that they were to treat him exactly as they treated himself.[5]

In the weeks that followed, Mr Noyes became a frequent visitor to the Continental Bank and handled thousands of pounds on behalf of his absent employer. The bank was completely satisfied with the arrangement and it seemed to be working well.

Meanwhile, on 17 January 1873, the busy Mr Warren did

manage to get away from Birmingham and pay another visit in person to the Bank of England branch at Burlington Gardens. However, both Mr Fenwick and Colonel Francis were shocked when they saw him. He looked terribly ill. He had a bandage on his face and his mobility was restricted severely. In fact, he was just about able to walk with the assistance of a walking stick. When they enquired of him what had happened, he told them that he had suffered a bad fall from his horse. Nevertheless, he was as eager as ever to do business. In his possession, he told them, he had a bill of exchange drawn on the Rothschild Bank, which he placed on the desk, declaring, with mock pride, 'There, I suppose that is good enough paper for you.'[6] Colonel Francis examined the bill and was indeed impressed:

> It was drawn on the London House of Messrs. Rothschild, in
> St. Swithin's-lane, and was duly marked as accepted ...[7]

Mr Warren informed them that 'though wanting rest very much', he would be going back to Birmingham again soon to 'arrange about his workshops'.[8] He had, he said, three different factory premises to choose from in Birmingham and he hoped to have his workshops in full operation, manufacturing the sleeping cars, by 1 February 1873.[9] As Mr Warren hobbled gingerly out of the bank, everything he had told the bank officials left them with the comforting impression that his business was progressing exceedingly well.

After that visit, the bills of exchange began to arrive from Birmingham with even greater rapidity and frequency. On 21 January 1873, Mr Warren sent in bills of exchange to the value of £4,250. As always, he enclosed a letter to Colonel Francis:

Birmingham
21st January 1873

Dear Sir,
I hand you herewith, as per enclosed, memorandum bills for discount, the proceeds of which please place to my credit.
F. A. Warren[10]

Colonel Francis replied to his American friend and, following his recent appearance at the bank, asked about the state of his health:

> Western Branch of the Bank of England,
> London, January 22, 1873
>
> F. A. Warren, Esq., P. O. Birmingham:
>
> Dear Sir, – Your favour of the 21st, enclosing £4,250 in bills for discount, is received, and proceeds of same passed to your credit as requested. Hoping you are recovering from the effects of the fall from your horse, and that I may have the pleasure of seeing you in London soon, I remain, dear sir,
> Yours faithfully,
> P. M. Francis[11]

To a letter dated 12 February 1873, along with more enclosed bills of exchange, Mr Warren added a postscript answering Colonel Francis's kind comments of concern about the condition of his health:

> The mail was so near closing when I wrote my last that I did not have the time to make a proper acknowledgement of your good wishes in my behalf ... I inform you that I am gradually but slowly recovering, and also am succeeding thus far in matters of business to my wish.[12]

And again on 20 February 1873:

> I am happy to inform you that my doctor reports me as doing finely, with the prospect, should no drawback occur, of resuming my active life again in a few days. Under these circumstances I hope soon to have the pleasure of seeing you ...[13]

Whatever problems he had with his physical health, it was clear to the bankers that Mr Warren was doing well financially. Between 21 January and 28 February 1873, he sent Colonel Francis over ninety bills of exchange for discount. They came from some of the most prestigious financial institutions in the world including Rothschild, the Anglo-Austrian Bank, the International Bank of Hamburg, Suse and Sibeth, the Bank of Belgium and Holland, Baring Brothers, and the London and Westminster Bank. It came to the impressive amount of over £102,000, all paid over to Mr Warren and none of it due to be recouped by the bank until the bills began maturing.

CHAPTER 3

A Clerical Error

---·•·---

Friday 28 February 1873 began like any other at the Western branch of the Bank of England in Burlington Gardens. Among the items to be attended to that day were a batch of bills of exchange that had arrived from Birmingham to be credited to the account of Mr Warren. They had been received in the post, as usual, by Colonel Francis along with a letter dated the day before:

> Dear Sir,
> Enclosed I hand you memo. with bills for discount, proceeds of which please place to the credit of my account on receipt. I have yours of the 25th, acknowledging receipt of bills sent on 24th.
>   I remain, dear sir, yours faithfully,
>   F. A. Warren
>
> P.S. My dear Sir, I take this opportunity of thanking you for the trouble you have taken in my behalf in making special application to the Bank committee about the Anglo-Austrian and Russian Bank bills. I have some of each to the amount of about 6,000l., and shall either get two endorsements on them or return them to my friends. Accept, dear Sir, the assurance of my esteem, while I remain yours faithfully, F.A.W.[1]

The value of the bills enclosed on this occasion came to around £26,000[2]; a large amount, undoubtedly, but such were Mr Warren's business activities that the staff at the bank were accustomed to seeing amounts of that size making their way in and out of his account. The bills of exchange were dispatched, as usual, to the discount department and the clerk there went through each of them routinely but diligently.

The clerk then noticed that two of the bills, made out on the banking firm of Blydenstein & Co. for £1,000 each, were missing their dates of acceptance. He examined the bills closely. They were both written in French, drawn by D.L. Goldschmidt on B.W. Blydenstein and accepted by them. The endorsements of Carl Wolff, F.A. Warren and B.W. Blydenstein were also on them.[3]

The Bank of England clerk felt sure that the missing dates were nothing more than a clerical error that could be easily rectified by Blydenstein's, the London house of which was situated over in Great St Helen's. Mr Warren had an opening balance of £20,000 in his account that morning, which the value of the new bills brought to £46,000. The clerk placed the bills of exchange that were without any problem into the bank vault and those two with the missing dates he passed on to a messenger, with instructions that they be taken round to Blydenstein's as soon as possible for the insertion of the relevant information. As a matter of course, Colonel Francis was informed that there was a slight 'hitch' regarding two of Mr Warren's bills of exchange.

Later that same day the messenger set off for Blydenstein's with the bills. It wasn't long before he returned with the startling news that the staff at Blydenstein's had found more wrong with the bills than merely the missing dates. In fact, he said, they had declared them to be worthless forgeries. The officials there told him that they had never used a stamp like the one used across these bills, which read 'Accepted at the London Joint Stock Bank'. Furthermore, Mr D.L. Goldschmidt never drew on their bank at all. This news caused instant shock to reverberate around the Burlington branch of the Bank of England. Nevertheless, a hurried examination of Mr Warren's financial records with the bank reassured the officials that there must be some mistake: surely the staff at Blydenstein's had got something wrong? After all, this was Mr Warren they were talking about, whom they knew to be a rich American industrialist, a customer of the bank for some months now and over in England to further his interests in the lucrative railway industry. He was a friend of Colonel Francis and Mr Fenwick. His account showed a healthy flow of funds and, furthermore, all those who had met him believed him to be a respectable young man who was the perfect example of an American gentleman.

Mr Fenwick had no doubts that he was a reputable businessman. He remembered the sleeping cars and how Mr Warren had said that he would soon have the English tourists travelling to Vienna in them, the three different factories in Birmingham that he had to choose from and his other inventions such as the signal light for the front of railway engines. Colonel Francis concurred: Mr Warren had come over from America 'to introduce sundry American inventions, first and foremost of which were the sleeping-cars, and some others'.[4] Of course, both men had a lot of professional pride and reputation riding on the question of whether their faith in Mr Warren had been justified.

Nevertheless, no matter what Colonel Francis and Mr Fenwick thought, an innocent answer could not be found to explain Blydenstein's insistence that the bills were forgeries. The police were sent for. As heated and frantic discussions took place between the bank officials and the police, the work of the branch proceeded in as normal a way as possible in an attempt to present a calm and orderly front to the general public. Rumours that a fraud had been committed upon the seemingly impenetrable Bank of England would spread quickly around the city and could even become reflected in dealings on the financial markets.

Those at the bank, when prompted by police questioning, began to ask who Mr Frederick Albert Warren really was. How much did they know about him? Was he all that he seemed? More of the bills of exchange that Mr Warren had posted to Colonel Francis for discount were sent for validation and they kept coming back rejected as forgeries. Very soon the scale of what was occurring became immense. It began to look as if the Bank of England had handed out a vast sum of money, over £102,000, and all they had got in return was a stack of useless forged bills of exchange.

CHAPTER 4

Arrest at the Continental Bank

————•—•—————

A s the hours passed and the staff at the Bank of England dug frantically into the financial affairs of Mr Frederick Albert Warren, a link was found to exist between his account and that of Mr C.J. Horton at the Continental Bank. Consequently, Frank May, deputy cashier at the Bank of England, was dispatched to the Continental Bank on the following morning, Saturday 1 March, to make enquiries regarding Mr Horton. As it happened, at around 1 p.m., while Mr May was actually at the Continental Bank, the young American known to the staff as Mr Horton's clerk arrived to transact some business. Mr Noyes was pointed out to Mr May, who approached him immediately and quizzed him about the matter. Mr Noyes was alarmed: 'When I got to the bank with a check for £5,000, I found myself in a moment surrounded by bank officials and detectives.'[1] Mr Noyes told those gathered around him that he knew nothing about any forged bills being presented at the Bank of England. He told them that he was an employee of Mr Horton's and was ignorant of the more intimate details of the man's business dealings. He did offer to go and get Mr Horton for them but, understandably, was not allowed to go anywhere. In fact Mr May, on behalf of the Bank of England, asked that he be taken into custody by the police immediately. As Noyes continued to protest his innocence, this was done by city policeman Jonathan Pope.

'You are given into custody on a charge of fraud upon the Bank of England,' Constable Pope informed the American.

'You have no right to take me without a warrant,' protested Noyes. 'Where is your warrant?'

The policeman told him that no warrant was required in this situation and that he must accompany him immediately to the police station in Bow Lane.

The staff at the Continental Bank were just as confident about the honesty of Mr Horton and Mr Noyes as their counterparts at the Bank of England had been about Mr Warren. Mr C.J. Horton was a respected and important client of the Continental Bank and the manager told the police that he was prepared to vouch personally for Mr Noyes as Mr Horton's clerk. Richard Amery, ledger keeper at the bank, said that he knew the young American, Edwin Noyes; that he paid cash frequently into the account of his employer, Mr C.J. Horton, and also cashed cheques on the account. They were all satisfied that this arrangement had been put in place correctly and everything was legitimate. On the other hand, this young American was the only lead that the police had and they were not going to let him go that easily. There was no sign of Mr Warren or Mr Horton and neither were proving easy to contact.

As they made their way to the police station, Mr Noyes continued to tell the police that he was innocent of any crime and that they had the wrong man in custody.

'You had better take me to Mr Horton's,' he told them.

'Where are Mr Horton's rooms?' asked Constable Pope.

'At the Cannon Street Hotel,' answered Noyes. 'You had better take me there, and he will make all things right.'[2]

Pope told him that they would contact Mr Horton themselves.

When Pope searched Mr Noyes, he found a number of interesting items on him including 'an open check for 100*l*., drawn by Horton on the Continental Bank, two bank notes for 100*l*. and 10*l*., a gold watch and chain, a diamond ring, and a number of memoranda'.[3] He also found the document drawn up between Mr Noyes and Mr Horton whereby Noyes had agreed to become Horton's clerk. This referred to the £300 paid by Noyes to Horton. There were also a number of letters, some of which purported to be from Mr Horton to Mr Noyes, and some others referring to the advertisement that he had placed in the *Daily Telegraph* regarding the position of clerk. All of this seemed to back up Noyes' story. However, Noyes had given the police

Durrants Hotel as his address and when they checked this out they discovered that he had not been there for three weeks.

Noyes was brought to the Mansion House to appear before the Lord Mayor. As he waited for his turn to appear before his lordship, Noyes was challenged by Sergeant John Spittle of the city police about the discrepancy regarding his address.

'Mr Noyes, at the police station you gave your address as Durrants Hotel ... That is false, as you have left there these three weeks; the last meal you had there was on the 4th of last month; will you give me your correct address?'

'Who are you?' Noyes asked.

'I belong to the police. Now will you give it me?'

'No, I have no settled address, I have been stopping at different places.'

'Will you say where you slept last night?'

'No, after the manner I have been treated; if I had the opportunity I might be able to find Horton.'[4]

Noyes went on to claim that he had only given the address of Durrants Hotel because that is what Mr Horton had told him to do and because he had intended to return there. He continued to claim that, if they allowed him to go, he would be able to find Mr Horton and bring him to them to settle the whole affair. Once again the police declined his offer.

The authorities decided to go public with the story of the bank fraud in order to mitigate the effect of any forged documents that might still be in circulation. *The Times* newspaper on Monday 3 March warned all 'bankers, brokers, and others not to accept, receive, negotiate, or otherwise deal with any of the under mentioned securities of the United States, they, it is alleged, having been acquired out of the profits of the forgery ...'[5] It listed the serial numbers and amounts of these suspect bonds. The public and the banking profession were warned of how good the forgeries used in this case actually were:

> The forged bills are said to have been admirably executed, the signatures, the print, the paper, the stamps, &c., having been so carefully counterfeited as almost to defy detection.[6]

A £500 reward was offered for 'the apprehension of Frederick Albert Warren on the charge of forgery', also known as C.J. Horton.[7] He was described as being 'about 40 years of age, 5ft. 9in. or 10in. in height, thin, dark, and sallow, with dark hair and eyes'; as speaking with a strong American accent, and dressing 'fairly well in a frock coat and a loose brown overcoat'. In their edition of 4 March 1873, *The Times* confirmed for its readers that the fraudster had, to all appearances, 'succeeded in safely pocketing about a hundred thousand pounds'. They were concerned about 'the evidence it affords of the dangers to which our elaborate system of commercial finance is necessarily exposed'.[8]

CHAPTER 5

The Investigation Continues

The police did not believe that Noyes was the innocent dupe he was claiming to be and the fact that he was an American meant that Clarence A. Seward, the Bank of England's legal agent in New York, was asked to look into the matter on that side of the Atlantic. Seward hired the Pinkerton National Detective Agency, an organization that had been credited with making many high-ranking arrests over there. In fact William Pinkerton, who had been in London pursuing another case a few months earlier, remembered that he had spotted two of America's leading forgers in a tailor's shop there one day. He had warned the English police about their presence at the time. He was now able to supply much valuable information. Two Pinkerton detectives were dispatched to London immediately to help with the investigation. Meanwhile, attempts were continuing to get Noyes to talk truthfully about his role in the affair. There were rumours that he had even been visited in person by Lionel de Rothschild, on behalf of the board of directors of the Bank of England, who offered him his freedom and £1,000 in return for everything he knew about the forgeries. This story was later denied by the bank, but Noyes himself always claimed that something like that had actually happened:

> ... a high official of the bank of England ... offered me £1,000 and a free pardon if I would 'round on' my accomplices.[1]

Noyes stuck doggedly to his story about being nothing more than an innocent employee of Mr Horton's, who knew nothing about the finer details of the man's finances. This was a serious high-profile crime and the police were working hard on getting it solved. The authorities at the Bank of England were concerned about the damage that had been done to their reputation as a secure financial institution and they were prepared to use their extensive financial resources in order to repair that damage and get revenge on those responsible. Noyes' clothes were traced to a particular tailor in London. When the detectives visited the company they found out that a man had purchased the garments there under the name of Mr Bedford. One of the salesmen remembered that he had seen this Mr Bedford walking in Mayfair one day in the company of another man. The detectives undertook a door-to-door investigation in Mayfair and found a witness who identified the man who had been seen walking with the prisoner that day as a patient of Dr Payson Hewett, of No. 1, Mayfair. The detectives then questioned the doctor in question, but all he knew was that the man had given his address as the Westminster Palace Hotel. He did remember that the man said he was 'a medical graduate from an American university' and, as 'he had a perfect knowledge of medical subjects', the doctor found his story credible. The police went to the Westminster Palace Hotel but the trail went cold when it transpired that no such man had ever been a guest there.

Only hours after his arrest at the Continental Bank, Mr Noyes found himself standing before no less a person than the Lord Mayor of London, Sir Sydney Waterlow, at the Mansion House. He was accused of a most serious crime. It would be for the Lord Mayor to decide, following an examination of the evidence, whether the American had charges to answer and whether he would, ultimately, be sent for trial at the Old Bailey. The Lord Mayor declared that for particular reasons he would invoke a statute under which he was entitled to hold the examination of the prisoner in private. He took this course of action, most likely, because of pressure from the Bank of England, who did not want to expose its shortcomings in public. It was a decision, however, that brought the Lord Mayor in for a lot of criticism. It meant that anyone without a direct connection to the case had to leave the courtroom. The ruling applied not only to members of the public but also to the newspaper correspondents who, understandably, felt highly aggrieved.

The hearing then commenced at which the bank was represented by the company's solicitor, Mr Freshfield, while Noyes had no legal representation at all. Frank May, deputy chief cashier of the Bank of England, was called as a witness and he stated in his evidence that it had been brought to his notice on the night before, Friday 28 February 1873, that a number of forged bills had been submitted for discount at their branch located at Burlington Gardens. He said that he found out that at least some of the funds from the account of the individual who submitted the forged bills had been paid into an account at Continental Bank in Lombard Street and he went there that very day, Saturday, to make inquiries regarding the matter. It was from the staff there that he first found out about Mr Noyes who, they said, acted as a clerk on behalf of Mr Horton. Mr May explained to the Lord Mayor that, as it happened, the prisoner actually came into the bank while he was there and was pointed out to him as the said Mr Noyes. Mr May told the court that he then had the man detained on suspicion of involvement in the fraud.

Richard Amery, ledger keeper at the Continental Bank, was called to give evidence and said that he knew the prisoner, Mr Noyes, as the man who handled all the banking affairs of Mr C.J. Horton. A cheque was produced in court as an example of the kind of transaction that Noyes usually engaged in at the Continental Bank. This particular cheque was made out for £6,000, dated 25 February 1873, drawn on the Western branch of the Bank of England, signed 'F. A. Warren' and made payable to 'Thomas Carter'. It was endorsed 'Thos. Carter' and 'C. J. Horton'. Mr Amery told the Lord Mayor that Noyes had deposited the cheque in Mr Horton's account and the amount was duly paid over by the Bank of England.[2]

The next witness called was Colonel Francis, who was able to confirm that this cheque for £6,000 was indeed paid by his branch of the Bank of England in Burlington Gardens on 28 February 1873. He also testified that the bank account from which the funds had been drawn had been opened by a Mr Frederick Albert Warren in the preceding May. A letter was produced in evidence, dated 27 February 1873, sent by Mr Warren to Colonel Francis. It was the most recent letter he had received from Mr Warren and had been accompanied by a batch of the forged bills. The Lord Mayor heard that the value of the bills sent in on that occasion came to £26,000. Mr William Henry Trumpler, from the bank of B.W. Blydenstein, testified before the Lord Mayor that his company had declared two of those bills to be forgeries.

Detective Sergeant Spittle told of his initial interview with the prisoner, Mr Noyes, on the morning of the prisoner's detention at the Continental Bank and his subsequent refusal to give any address except Durrants Hotel from where, it later transpired, he had moved some weeks earlier.

Having heard all this damning evidence presented against the prisoner, the Lord Mayor was satisfied, for the moment, that Mr Noyes had a case to answer; he remanded him in custody until the following Friday when the examination would continue. By now the news of this audacious financial crime had spread and the security procedures of the Bank of England were coming under severe scrutiny; the bank authorities were forced to explain how a momentous breach of this kind had occurred. They insisted that they had always 'exercised very great caution in admitting new customers to the privilege of obtaining discount'.[3] They attempted to make their position clear:

Any person who desires to open a 'discount account' must be introduced by one of the Directors, and, consequently, very careful inquiries are made into his respectability and solvency.[4]

One excuse given for what had happened was that the West End branch located at Burlington Gardens was 'an entirely different kind of business from the parent establishment in the City' and was 'intended for the convenience of gentlemen and ladies and West End tradesmen who might find it inconvenient to journey to the City in order to transact their occasional business'.[5] The bank authorities were arguing, therefore, that the branch was not 'ordinarily concerned with the large bill transactions of City commerce'. In other words, they were trying to lay the blame for this calamity on the naivety of Colonel Francis and his staff at that particular branch.

The press were intrigued with the details of the case, the large sum of money defrauded and the identities of the characters involved. *The Times* outlined the calmness and meticulous planning with which the mysterious Mr F.A. Warren, in particular, had carried out his fraudulent business:

> He behaved for some time just like an ordinary customer of good resources. He drew upon his balance and renewed it, but kept it always at a good figure. After a while he deposited some bills. They were good and genuine bills. Still he was careful not to be hasty, and he continued his transactions with the Bank until he had acquired the reputation of a person engaged in legitimate commerce and thoroughly trustworthy. At length the moment came for the presentation of the Forged Bills. They were discounted without hesitation.[6]

The criminal actions of the forgers were described in *The Times* as 'masterpieces of ingenuity and patience'.[7] The correspondent could not help marvelling at the artistry of someone capable of forging financial documents in such a professional manner:

> In the first place, many of the large firms upon whom the Bills purported to be drawn are in the habit of using a peculiar kind of paper, with certain water-marks and printed matter. All this would have to be imitated, and, as the Bills were drawn on more than one firm there must have been several such imitations. There remained the drawing of the Bills and the affixing the signatures, and each Bill must have required a series of feats in successful forging. Some Bills were backed by several acceptors, so that there might easily be as many as half-a-dozen signatures on a single Bill. Yet the Bills were so perfect that not one of them was questioned on the ground of the acceptances not appearing genuine. The plot had, to all appearance, a success which its consummate skill and patience deserved.[8]

The writer pondered on why people possessing such obvious talents would opt to use them in this deviant manner:

It is not the work of an ordinary thief who might forge to obtain the immediate necessities of life. It is more like the desperation of gamblers ... who find pleasure in staking everything they have on a mere chance.[9]

CHAPTER 6

Noyes at the Mansion House for the Second Time

Edwin Noyes was returned to the Mansion House for a second time at twelve o'clock on the following Friday, 7 March. To onlookers he now appeared 'anxious and dejected' and, compared to the first time they had seen him just under a week earlier, 'much altered in appearance for the worse'.[1] It was already clear that the authorities were not choosing to regard him as some kind of innocent dupe in the affair. In fact, the initial charge brought against him was the very serious one of 'fraudulently obtaining £4,500 by means of documents alleged to have been forged, and by conspiring with other persons, at present unknown, with intent to defraud the Governor and Company of the Bank of England'.[2] His age was given in court as twenty-nine years and he was described in the newspaper as being 'a citizen of the United States, and of gentlemanly appearance'.[3] To underline the serious nature of his predicament, on the bench beside the Lord Mayor sat Alfred de Rothschild, one of the directors of the Bank of England. Mr Freshfield once again represented the Bank of England while this time Noyes did have legal counsel in the person of Dr Kenealy QC.

The Lord Mayor permitted this second hearing to take place in open court and not in private as before. Dr Kenealy was voicing the majority view when he objected to the fact that the case against a man facing a criminal charge had been heard in private on the previous occasion and, furthermore, that the man had not been legally represented. He went so far as to compare the proceedings of the first day to the workings of the

Inquisition.[4] This emotive language forced the Lord Mayor to defend himself:

> The prisoner had then been in custody only a few hours; there was at that time reason to believe that an enormous fraud had been committed, and that the ends of justice might be frustrated if the circumstances were made public at the first hearing ... Although the prisoner was not represented by counsel on the first occasion, the Lord Mayor took good care, in the discharge of his duty, to see that he was in no way prejudiced by the manner in which the investigation was conducted.[5]

Not only was the evidence that had been presented at the first hearing read out in open court by the chief clerk, Mr Oke, but Noyes' counsel was given the opportunity of cross-examining the witnesses who had given it.

Once the evidence from the first hearing had been put on the record in open court and Dr Kenealy was satisfied with proceedings, the work of the second day began. Colonel Francis was recalled to the stand and a number of letters and the amounts in forged bills received from Mr Warren on each date over the preceding months were read out. Mr May was also recalled and gave evidence that he had made inquiries regarding some of the bills sent in the last batch by 'Mr Warren'. He confirmed that 'those bills made payable to Messrs Rothschild, the London and Westminster Bank, and the Union Bank amounting to 12,000*l.* were forgeries'.[6] Mr Thomas Flower, of Rothschild's, said he himself had examined two £1,000 bills and he declared them both to be forgeries as well: 'They were imitations of the signature of Sir Anthony de Rothschild,' he said, 'but not good imitations.'[7]

Mr Alfred Joseph Baker, a clerk at Messrs Jay Cooke, McCulloch and Co., American bankers in Lombard Street, told of a transaction that had taken place there earlier on the Friday of Noyes' arrest. He told how Noyes had bought some bonds from them that day with cheques drawn by F.A. Warren on the Western branch of the Bank of England on behalf of Mr Horton. Mr Baker said that they were very familiar with Mr Noyes at Messrs Jay Cooke,

McCulloch and Co. and all their transactions with him had 'involved large sums of money'. This evidence showed a clear link between Noyes, the Horton account at the Continental Bank and the Warren account at the Bank of England:

> The firm had been sometimes paid with checks of Warren on the Western Branch of the Bank of England, and at other times with checks of Horton on the Continental Bank.[8]

Detective Sergeant Spittle and policeman Jonathan Pope described how the prisoner had been taken into custody on that Friday and brought to the police station. They also spoke of the various items that had been found on his person, including a letter from Mr Horton, in which Noyes was instructed to collect the money, 'go on with the business' and meet Mr Horton at Broad Street Station.

As the hearing drew to a close for the day, Mr Freshfield requested that the prisoner be remanded for a further week as, he argued, it was clear from the evidence 'that he had been dealing with very large sums of money, and acting almost in the character of a principal – certainly that of an accomplice'.[9] Dr Kenealy, on behalf of his client, objected to this and, on the contrary, submitted that Mr Noyes should be freed. He claimed that although Mr Noyes was clearly a clerk to Mr Horton, there was no proof at all that Mr Horton and Mr Warren were the same person. His client, he said, had nothing to do with this Mr Warren:

> What had Mr Noyes done more than a clerk of any merchant in the City? It might be assumed that bills proved afterwards to be forgeries often passed through the hands of innocent persons who had no knowledge of the risk they ran ... Noyes had advertised for a situation as clerk on coming to this country from America in December last, and ... he had no previous acquaintance with Horton. Was it likely if Horton was about to embark in a gigantic fraud, he would take a perfect stranger into his confidence?

This argument might have sounded reasonable but the Lord Mayor remained unconvinced about the prisoner's innocence:

> ... he was found dealing on one day with money amounting to 22,000*l*. the produce of forged bills, and ... a letter was found upon him asking him to bring the money to a person whom he would find in the first-class waiting room at a railway station.... the prisoner must have known the moneys with which he was dealing had been acquired by unlawful means.

Noyes was duly remanded for another week and sent back to Newgate Prison, where he was being held in custody.

It was only when Noyes' second hearing at the Mansion House was over that the public became aware for the first time that a big breakthrough had been made in the investigation. This revelation came about when the next case was called to be heard before the Lord Mayor: it concerned two people, a man and a woman, who were suspected of being involved in the Great Fraud on the Bank of England. Helen Vernon and Jules Meunier had been arrested the evening before, in possession of a bag of money, at Euston Station. The Lord Mayor was told how they had been detained at half past eight on Thursday evening, 6 March, with over £2,000 in gold. The police believed that the gold, contained inside a bag in their possession, was a portion of the proceeds from the Great Bank Fraud. Miss Helen Vernon, normally known as Nelly, was described in the newspaper as 'a fashionably-dressed young woman of 20' and Meunier as a thirty-four-year-old maker of musical instruments.[10]

Detective Sergeant Spittle, in his evidence, explained that he went to the train station that evening and saw the prisoners there with a leather bag, which turned out to be full of gold. When questioned, Meunier told the police that he knew nothing about the contents of the bag. The Belgian national claimed that Nelly Vernon was a friend of his wife's and that he had been asked by his wife if he could accompany her to Birmingham 'to take care of the property'. He had, he said, 'just received it from a man in a public house close by'.[11] Apart from that, he knew nothing about the money. Nelly confirmed to the police that what Mr

Meunier had said was true. She told them that Meunier got the bag from her husband and was simply asked to accompany her. For her own part, she said that she had been aware that the bag contained money, but not how much. Detective Sergeant Spittle confirmed that both prisoners had given their correct addresses when asked. Nelly 'begged' that Meunier 'be released on account of his family', saying that he 'was a very respectable man'.[12] He was, however, remanded for a week, although the Lord Mayor conceded 'that if the inquiries of the police as to the antecedents of the male prisoner were satisfactory he would admit him to bail'.[13]

In the end it turned out to be true that Meunier had nothing to do with the fraud. In fact, Nelly Vernon was not really involved as a principal either, but she was linked to the men who were the main protagonists. It was after the arrest of Nelly, who agreed to give evidence to protect herself, that three names became top priority for the police and the Bank of England. These names were George Bidwell, Austin Bidwell and George Macdonnell. As it happened, Austin Bidwell and Macdonnell were the American forgers who had been spotted in London by the detective William Pinkerton only a few months earlier.

The arrest of Nelly and Meunier was not the only development in the case; in the days that followed, the police located a woman they believed to be the mistress of their suspect Edwin Noyes. She admitted to having lived with him since 1 February 1873. What this woman, Ellen Franklin, told them about their prisoner confirmed what many of them thought: it cast serious, if not terminal, doubts on Noyes' claims to be innocent.

It was now imperative that these suspects be rounded up as quickly as possible, so the Lord Mayor issued warrants for the arrests of Mr George Bidwell, Mr Frederick Albert Warren, also known as Austin Bidwell, and Mr George Macdonnell. Background information and photographs were being sent from America. In addition, it was announced in *The Times* that £500 each would be offered as a reward for information leading to their apprehension and conviction. Austin Bidwell or Frederick Albert Warren, the paper said, also went by the names Horton, Pierce, Albretch, Walker, and Nelson; Macdonnell was known as Swift or Sweet;

while George Bidwell was 'otherwise Burton'.[14] Their descriptions were circulated:

> Macdonnell: Age 30, looks older; height 5 feet 10 to 11 inches; fair complexion, hair dark brown, inclined to baldness; wore beard and moustache; has scars on neck, under right ear; pimples on forehead, which is high; small blue eyes, strong build, gentlemanly in manner, speaks with a slight American accent, speaks English, French, German, and Italian; was lately lodging in St. James Place, Pall Mall.

> George Bidwell: Aged 40 to 42; height 5 feet 8 inches, black hair, eyes rather sunken, sallow complexion, whiskers and beard recently shaved off; rather strong built man, with short neck; supposed to wear brown mixture suit, probably an over-coat, and carried a black bag.

An earlier description given of Mr Warren was now amended to read:

> ... 30 to 35 years of age, but sometimes looks older; height, 6 feet; very thin and bony, had dark whiskers and moustache, hair black and wavy, eyes sunken, glassy appearance; shows teeth, speech rough and American; may be accompanied by a young woman, 18 to 20 years of age, looks younger with golden hair.[15]

Both Warren and Macdonnell, *The Times* reported, were known to usually wear 'large diamond rings'.[16] By 15 March there was another update in the *London Illustrated News:*

> The Sum of £1500 is now offered as a reward for the appre-hension of the perpetrators of the great City forgeries. These persons, three in number, are described as Frederick Albert Warren, passing under the names of C. J. Horton, Austin Bidwell, Pierce, Frederic Albretch, Walker, and Nelson; George Macdonnell, alias Swift or Sweet; and George Bidwell, alias Burton. Detailed descriptions of the men have been circulated.

Edwin Noyes, the American who is charged with complicity in the forgeries perpetrated on the Bank of England, underwent his first public examination, yesterday week, at the Mansion House. A smaller case, arising out of this gigantic fraud, was afterwards heard. This was the charge against a man and woman for being in possession of a bag containing £2717 10s, in gold, supposed to be part of the proceeds of the forgeries. These two persons were also remanded for a week.[17]

In the months that followed, the British public were to find out a lot more about these three American criminals.

CHAPTER 7

The Bidwells

———•◦•———

The investigators were correct: the three individuals responsible for the Great Fraud on the Bank of England were the
brothers George Bidwell and Austin Biron Bidwell, along with
their criminal associate George Macdonnell. Edwin Noyes Hills
was a minor player in the affair. George, who was around forty
years of age in 1873, was the elder of the two Bidwell brothers
and the leader of this American criminal gang that had come over
to Europe in 1872 to ply its trade. His younger brother Austin,
twenty-seven in 1873, was the one who had played the roles of Mr
Frederick Albert Warren and Mr C.J. Horton so well.

George was born in Orleans County, New York, to strict
parents who had been young converts to the Methodist religion:

> We were debarred from playing with a kitten or a doll. A pack
> of cards in the house would (we were told) have brought down
> a judgement from Heaven upon us. Even the game of checkers
> was looked upon with suspicion, and regarded as a temptation
> of the devil.[1]

In 1837 the family moved to Michigan where their father set up in
business. Life there proved tough, however, with him failing to
thrive in business and, at one point, the whole family becoming
afflicted with an illness that led to the death of George and Austin's
two-year-old brother. It is quite obvious that George had business
instincts from a young age which, had things worked out differ-
ently, or had he been of a different temperament, could have
brought him success in the world of legitimate commerce. Instead,

he succumbed to what he called 'the gradual undermining' of his 'honest business principles'.[2] Having made the choice to involve himself in dishonest practices, George's influence then drew Austin in as well. Nevertheless, it does seem that without George's obvious business acumen, the family could, on a number of occasions, have perished.

When George was only nine years of age he supported the family financially by selling molasses, candy and apples during a period when their father was ill. At the age of eleven, in order to earn some money, he sawed and chopped up wood for a distant cousin. The cousin was so impressed with his work ethic that he offered to take George into his own family, provide him with an education and, eventually, set him up in business. George's parents, however, decided that it was most important that they attend to the boy's religious upbringing and so turned down the generous offer. 'I believe,' said George, 'this was an unfortunate decision for me.'[3] In 1845 the family moved to Toledo, Ohio, and the young George was soon back in business again, supporting the family until his father could get established. This time he sold 'periodicals and apples, trashy novels and candy, lemonade and pocket-knives, small-beer and steel watch-chains' all from a stall on the street.[4]

George managed to make sufficient profit from this enterprise to allow himself the small luxury of a twenty-three-foot-long sailing boat, the use of which soon became an enthralling passion of his. He spent his summer days away from home exploring the waterways of the locality. That was until the hull of his vessel needed some repair work and he took it to an old friend of his father's to have the work carried out. When it was complete the man presented him with a bill amounting to $18. The fifteen-year-old George had expected the carpenter, being a friend of his father's, to wait for the money but, much to his surprise, the man demanded immediate payment. George went to his father, who at that time was in reasonable financial stead, and asked him for a loan to tide him over. His father refused and the carpenter seized and sold George's prized boat. Although he hadn't realized it at the time, George later believed that a cruel conspiracy had been at play all along:

... I have since thought there was an arrangement between my father and the carpenter to get the boat away from me, and thus turn my energies in another direction.[5]

According to George, a recurring pattern in the lives of the Bidwell brothers was for some dishonourable character to inveigle his way into their father's confidence and business affairs and before long swindle him out of whatever money he had. Ironic, then, or perhaps understandable, that his sons became people who made a career of swindling others rather than being swindled themselves. Before long their father's pattern was repeated, the family business was lost and they were all thrown back into poverty.

In 1849, George and his father set off, in the middle of winter, on the long trek to Grand Rapids in search of their fortune. They had with them some borrowed money and the hope of starting a new business there. They managed to get through the snow, rent a shop and were soon making a profit. Later the whole family joined them. Over the next five years the Bidwells' candy business thrived and life, at last, became better. The father by now seemed to realize that George, although still only a teenager, was the superior businessman in the family and so began letting his son take the lead:

Now that I was at the helm, everything certainly prospered; home comforts increased; better educational advantages for the younger brothers and sisters were enjoyed.

I was highly respected by those members of the community whose good opinion was worth having; all of whom had unbounded confidence in my integrity and business capacity.[6]

Their shop did a good trade not only in candy but also in fancy goods and jewellery. It was then, however, that George's ambition led him into trouble for the first, although not the last, time in his life. The Bidwells, like all the other business people in the area, ordered their goods from the big wholesale suppliers in New York. George came up with the idea of going into the wholesale business himself and becoming a supplier of goods to the other stores in an area of up to 100 miles, but it soon ran into difficulties; in many areas the road network was so poor that the wear and tear on horses, wagons and goods was considerable. This was exacerbated by the fact that George had limited knowledge of business accounting and failed to manage the figures. When cash flow in the business became an issue and his debts rose, he didn't act quickly enough to jettison the wholesale business:

> ... that is exactly what an older head would have advised; and, as the rest of the business was profitable, it is likely I should have remained in Grand Rapids to this day.[7]

This situation was only aggravated by the unhelpful input of an inept, and perhaps unethical, lawyer. George went to this man for advice even though his practice was newly established in town and he didn't have any other clients. It proved a poor decision: 'When I explained the state of affairs he evidently saw that his opportunity had come, and he made the most of it.'[8] The lawyer advised George to place all the property that they owned into the possession of an assignee, following which it could be sold and the profits divided up among his creditors:

> ... those creditors who had shown me some attention when I had visited their places of business were put in the first class, to be paid in full out of the assets. The second class was composed of those who had favored me less. These came in next if enough were left to pay them. Under such an iniquitous arrangement the third class could of course receive nothing.[9]

George was later convinced that the lawyer only did this because he knew that such an arrangement would lead to those creditors in the second- and third-class assignments suing for equal treatment with those in the first, which would result in business for himself. In any event this is what happened, and it kept the lawyer busy for two years, while destroying George's business in the process: 'I look back to this assignment as the direct starting point of all my misfortunes.'[10]

As a result of this latest mishap, the Bidwell family was plunged back into poverty once again. When George was twenty-three years of age he decided, in despair, to leave for New York. At first, life in the big city was tough; he only had enough money to rent a cheap room in Greenwich Street and the most he could spend on food was twenty or twenty-five cents a day and later, when his financial situation had deteriorated even further, ten or fifteen cents. Eventually, though, through a contact in the grocery business, he managed to find employment. His new job entailed travelling around selling wholesale goods to grocery stores. It was work that he took to easily and he soon built up a respectable portfolio of clients. Although, unfortunately, the business folded, George was able to use his list of clients to secure a position with a rival grocery supplier.

Meanwhile, although the eldest son was doing better in New York, things were going from bad to worse for the family left at home. George managed to come up with a creative idea that might support them; he had salvaged $300 from the sale of some of his own personal property following the recent business failure and he used a substantial amount of that to buy sugar in New York and ship it back to his family at home. The plan was that they would use this to keep the candy business going. However, the creditors heard about this purchase of sugar and managed to have it treated as part of the assets of the failed business. The family was forced to relinquish it and so lost their last chance of saving the business.

The Bidwell parents then decided that they would move the whole family to a village called Muskegon, where they had been offered the opportunity to become involved in establishing a Methodist society and building a church. When he heard this news, it disturbed George greatly. He had heard of Muskegon and the bad reputation it had at that time. He worried that his parents didn't realize what they were leading the family into:

> In 1857, it was a village of wooden huts, cabins, and small houses, inhabited principally by lumber men and those 'tough and rough' characters usually found on the outskirts of civilization. Whisky-selling, gambling, dog-fighting, and more brutal animal bipeds bruising each other, was the order of the day.[11]

Nevertheless, there was nothing George could do about his parents' decision. They moved and, along with their religious work, opened a hotel in Muskegon. George's concerns were soon proved right. On many occasions, rather than paying their bill at the hotel, the customers would invite his father out onto the street for a fight to settle the matter. Mr Bidwell Senior was no fighter, however, and it was soon clear that there was no future for the family in Muskegon. Even though he was earning only $600 a year, George felt he had no other option but to take all of them to New York. He figured that his father could get a job and perhaps his brother, Austin, who was now twelve years of age, could work in an office. He rented a house in South Brooklyn for the whole family.

In 1858 George took up a new position for which he received a salary rather than a commission on sales as he had before. That same year, now in his mid twenties, he married his seventeen-year-old sweetheart. On a visit back to Connecticut he had fallen 'deeply in love' with this young woman. Although he knew that another mouth to feed was the last thing that he needed at that point in his life, the heart ruled:

> ... I feared that by delay I might lose the dear object of my affections. Therefore, I rashly cast all prudential considerations to the winds, a customary proceeding among lovers.[12]

The birth of a son followed. With such a large number of people to feed in hard times, it is not surprising that financial difficulties were soon troubling George again. The opportunity arose to set Austin up in a confectionery business, this time in partnership with a man who had access to some money. In the end, however, the business failed and it ended up costing the family more than it brought in.

They were now struggling to meet basic living costs in New York and George was forced to live on his wits. He decided, apparently for the first time in his life, to bend the rules. Part of his job with the wholesale company entailed collecting money from customers. He began to use that money to pay his own personal expenses, with the intention of making sure that the customers' accounts were settled in full at the end of the month. Of course, it was against the rules, but as long as the customers' bills were paid, no one was the wiser. It didn't take long for the scheme to go wrong: at the end of one particular month George found himself $15 short, which meant that some of the customers' bills had to go unpaid. The situation deteriorated over a number of months until George's employers, although they were unaware of it, were down by $250.

Just when it looked as if George's dishonest financial practices would be exposed, an old acquaintance from Grand Rapids arrived with a business proposition. The man had a new brand of coffee roaster and he wanted to sell half his share of the patent right. George liked the product and believed that he could success-fully sell it. Realizing that this could be a way to get out of trouble, he decided to buy the man out. George's instincts about the coffee roaster proved correct and it sold well. So well, in fact, that he was soon able to sell half of his share to another businessman for $1,500. He was able to pay off his debt to his employers and no one noticed his dodgy accounting practices. Soon afterwards he moved to another employer and continued to work on the coffee roaster business in his own time.

George, however, had made a mistake. His former employers were contacted by an irate customer in Willimantic who complained that he had been billed for $10 that he had already paid over to George Bidwell. Furthermore, he said, he had a receipt in his possession to prove it. The problem was that the old employers had no record of ever receiving the money. When he was chal-lenged on the matter, George explained that it was merely a clerical error and he sent them the $10 to settle the account. The owners of the company, however, were not happy with his explanation; they suspected that the discrepancy of $10 might represent only one small part of a larger dishonesty. They called the authorities and George Bidwell had his first brush with the law when he was arrested and charged with financial misappropriation. The case was brought to a hearing but, luckily for George, his former employers were unable to unearth any further instances of finan-cial irregularity on his behalf. He continued to claim vehemently that the matter was nothing more than an innocent clerical error.

After all, he told the justice, he had repaid the amount in full as soon as he was told about it. The justice accepted his story and no further action was taken. George's old bosses were still not satisfied with his explanation and, even though they couldn't pin anything on him legally, they met with his new employers and made them aware of their suspicions. The result was that George was sacked from his job.

His old company's act of revenge had deprived George of his regular income and, with the whole family now relying on him for support, he had to act quickly. He managed to find a partner and together they reopened an old but once successful bakery shop in Grand Street, New York. Money was scarce, however, and George was forced to make changes such as selling the lease he held on the house in Brooklyn and moving everyone to a tenement house elsewhere in New York. Although the bakery had once been very profitable, with no experience to draw on George and his partner failed to make a success of it and within a few months they were forced to close.

Other legitimate business enterprises followed such as a confectionery business in Broadway, the invention of an improved steam kettle and, at one point, the hiring of a warehouse in Toronto. There was very little success and eventually George found himself operating, once again, on the wrong side of the law. He became involved in a scam organized by a printer called Hilton by which credit notes were used to buy goods that were never paid for. George always claimed that he was nothing more than an innocent dupe in the enterprise and that, in fact, it destroyed his reputation in the business community. The truth is that, from then on, criminality became his way of life.

His involvement with crime grew more serious when he became associated with a criminal called Frank Kibbe. In George's own opinion it was an association that proved to be crucial: 'my acquaintance with that man proved the most unfortunate event of my life.'[13] They began running fraudulent scams together, buying goods with credit notes that they never had any intention of honouring. In the end, according to George, Kibbe ran out on him owing him a lot of money. After an extensive search, George did manage to trace him to Buffalo and had him arrested by the police.

But then, according to George, the police doubled-crossed him, took a bribe from Kibbe and let him go free again. He finally caught up with Kibbe in Canada and this time managed to get $2,400 out of him in cash and $8,000 in products such as flour, beef, pork, lard, oil and butter, which he knew he could sell. He knew that this was all he was going to get from his unscrupulous friend.

After that matters did not improve for George and he fell in with yet another seasoned crook. This time his accomplice was a man called Samuel Bolivar, who had not only passed himself off as a physician more than once but also had experience in professions as diverse as match peddler, canal driver, circus tumbler and printer's devil.[14] Their unscrupulous activities together eventually led them into considerable trouble. In 1864, for the first time in his life, George was convicted of fraud and sentenced, along with Bolivar, to two years in a West Virginia county gaol. He managed to escape, however, having only served eight months of his sentence, when he and a number of others removed the bars from the gaol window.

George's area of criminal expertise became fraud and forgery and, as his involvement in professional crime developed, his brother Austin was drawn into this world as well. Austin took to the profession of fraud so well that, at the end of his life, he was described by *The New York Times* as 'one of the most remarkable criminals ... this country has produced'.[15] His development as a criminal happened slowly. Born in 1846, as a young boy he worked at a sugar brokers in New York.[16] Later he got a job with a firm of financial brokers on Wall Street.[17] While there, he learned the techniques of financial trading and began to enjoy the lifestyle that the easy flow of money brought. He also learned how easily one could live the high life on credit. For someone who had such religious parents, it was a completely new world for him:

> ... I went to board at the old St. Nicholas, the then fashionable hotel. From that time I began to drift more and more away from home influences.[18]

He set up an enterprise with a young man from a wealthy family, Ed Weed, and they began to trade for themselves. For a while it was a profitable, if hectic, lifestyle:

The years ... were fortunate ones for Wall Street, stocks of
every kind on the boom, the general wealth of the country
massing up by leaps and bounds, and every kind of speculative
enterprise being launched. Our firm history was the usual one
of broker firms in that tumultuous arena – the Wall Street of
those days – commissions in plenty, a large income, but one's
bank account was never growing, for what was made by day
in the wild excitement of shifting values was thrown away
amid wilder scenes at night.[19]

In reality, however, Austin and Ed's trading business only managed
to survive the excesses of Wall Street, more than once, by means of
cash injections received from his business partner's rich father. In
the end their partnership was dissolved; Ed Weed's health having
failed, he sailed with his family on a trip to Europe during which
he died. Austin was left with nothing and before long would join
his brother in the world of confidence tricks, fraud and forgery.
George always felt responsible for having led Austin from being 'a
fine steady young man ... universally regarded as one likely to fill
an honourable position in the world' to being a convicted criminal.[20] It is true that once he reached his early teens George was
more of an influence on Austin than their parents:

My father had lost his grip on the world but his faith in the
Unseen remained. My mother, caring little for this life, lived in
and for the spiritual ...
   We loved our mother, but her soul was too gentle to keep in
restraint hot, fiery youth like my brothers and myself.[21]

In the beginning George took his brother into his illegal schemes
with the vain hope that he would not realize what was going on.
Eventually, though, George knew that Austin's 'eyes became
opened'.[22] Austin's own account of his life, on the other hand,
seems to show that he himself was largely responsible for the path
he chose. According to him, one of the first big fraud jobs with
which he was involved was the sale of some stolen US bonds in
Europe for a group of corrupt New York policemen. They had
approached him, it seems, because of his knowledge of financial

trading. Apart from noticing that Europe had no railway sleeping cars, it was while on this trip that Austin discovered something else that would be useful in later years:

> One great advantage a dishonest man had at that date in Europe, especially an American, was that if he dressed well they considered he must be a gentleman, and if he had money that was a proof of respectability – one they never thought of questioning, nor how he came by it; ... it was an article of their creed that all Americans are rich.[23]

The scheme passed off without a hitch and he made a good profit from it. After that other frauds followed until it became his normal way of life. He and George worked together successfully on a number of scams. Austin's appearance and manner always proved a great advantage. He possessed 'a pleasing personality' and 'a thorough knowledge of business'.[24] These were the qualities he used so effectively to charm Colonel Francis and the others at the Bank of England. Then there was his knowledge of the world of finance and banking that came from having worked on Wall Street. He was a quick learner, a good talker and someone with the kind of personality that people found trustworthy, which is always an attribute invaluable to the professional fraudster.

Exactly how many of George's forgery scams Austin had been involved with is hard to be sure of as George, especially in later years, tried to keep his name out of them.[25] They were part of a group of swindlers that operated in New York out of a headquarters in Broad Street.[26] The authorities believed that Austin was the person who had made off with $10,000 of other people's money from Cincinnati some years prior to 1873, having for a time appeared to his victims to be a perfectly legitimate businessman.[27] He was thought to have been involved with George in financial swindles carried out in New Orleans, Wheeling, New York, Brooklyn and Boston. In 1869 the law caught up with them both when Austin got two years in Sing Sing Penitentiary in New York and George got five years in the Massachusetts Penitentiary. Austin served his full sentence in Sing Sing while George got a pardon. George, it was believed, went to Michigan afterwards to work as a preacher, a profession he often used as a cover in times of need.[28]

By the 1870s they had established links with a group of the most accomplished professional forgers then working in America, people such as Walter Sheridan and George Engles. According to Austin they also worked with a number of corrupt New York policemen. He claimed that these policemen were kept informed of what they were involved in and received a percentage of the ensuing profits in return for help and hopefully 'impunity' if anything went wrong.[29]

By 1872 the Bidwells were about to take on a new challenge across the sea …

CHAPTER 8

A Trip To Europe

———•◦•———

To anyone who met the Bidwell brothers as they headed to Europe in 1872, they would have seemed the epitome of the rich American tourist, but this was no grand tour, long-deserved holiday or pleasure trip. This journey was taken, as George puts it, 'with a view of "raising the wind" out of European capitalists'.[1] Men of the Bidwells' criminal experience knew that the trip would require more than just two people to carry it out effectively. Consequently, joining them was their associate, George Macdonnell, known to his friends as Mac. Mac was a serious criminal, in his later twenties at the time, and a long-time close friend of the Bidwells.

Mac had an unusual background for one engaged in professional crime, coming from a respectable American family of Scottish-Irish descent. His mother claimed a direct line of descent from the O'Neills, the ancient kings of Ireland. Mac was born, near Boston, in 1846.[2] He was, at one time, a potential candidate for the Catholic priesthood with the Jesuits.[3] He was described as an 'accomplished scholar' who could speak a number of languages and had the conversational abilities to match. Austin was one of those who held him in high esteem:

> ... his billiant scholarship, elegant speech, logical force and fiery enthusiasm, made a most fascinating companion... . Mac's mind was a storehouse of erudition, his memory a picture gallery, whose chambers were gilded and decorated with many a glowing canvas.[4]

Mac's relatively affluent background meant that he may even have been sent to Harvard at one point to study medicine. In 1872 his parents were living 'in good circumstances' in Canada where his father was 'reported to be a large holder of real estate in Montreal'.[5]

All this time Mac's mother seemed to be in denial regarding his criminal ways, as demonstrated by the fact that she saw him off on this latest trip to Europe, choosing to believe that he was going away on business.[6] There was no doubt that he was a worthy addition to the Bidwell gang, or for that matter any criminal gang, being 'a remarkably shrewd, intelligent man' who 'had a wonderful power of telling a great deal without committing himself'. It was said that, at one time, before he became exposed in the United States as a crook, he was held in high esteem by many people: 'there was scarcely a moneyed man in New York, London, or Paris but would have given him aid and assistance in the largest transactions'.[7]

Whatever sentimental feelings Mac may have inherited for the old country of Ireland from his mother did not deter him from plying his illegal trade there. He went on a trip to Ireland in the autumn of 1871, along with Austin, and the two American gents altered a Bank of Ireland cheque for £3 so that it read £3,000. They then proceeded to cash the cheque in Belfast and, no doubt, had a most enjoyable stay in Mac's ancestral homeland on the proceeds. They went from there to Manchester where they continued to pass altered cheques and, by using a completely forged letter of introduction, managed to induce the banking firm owned by Messrs Heywood to part with what was described as 'a large sum'.[8]

Mac and one of the Bidwells, most likely Austin, were involved in an elaborate scam upon the jewellers, Tiffany & Co., in New York in 1867. In October of that year they rented rooms on Fifth Avenue from a physician called James W. Barnard.[9] Mac, playing the role of an English gent, Henry B. Livingston, who was on holiday in New York, told the doctor that he was tired of hotels and wanted somewhere more comfortable to stay while he was in the city. It all sounded very reasonable when Mr Livingston told it. Naturally, Mr Livingston had his valet, Clarence, along with him, a role played by Austin. The fact that the rooms were expensive was not a problem for Mr Livingston and he agreed to pay an amount in advance. Two hours later, Mr Livingston and Clarence made their way to Tiffany's. By this time, however, Mac was no longer speaking like an Englishman and when he was asked for his name he said it was W.H. Barnard of Fifth Avenue, a son of the well-known physician. He caused no suspicion at Tiffany's; he was their typical fussy customer. He perused the valuable goods for some time before settling upon a number of items that he wanted to buy: 'a solitaire ring, a brooch with seven stones, two diamond ear-drops and two large unset diamonds.'[10] The value came to almost $2,500. He would go and see Daddy, he told the staff, and return in two hours with the money.

When he returned two hours later, there was a slight problem: he had not actually met his father, but had got word to him to have the money left at the house. If the salesman could come with him to the house, with the valuables, he would pay him then. He pointed to his impressive coach and horses outside, driven by a man he referred to as Charles.[11] The salesman agreed and off they set for Fifth Avenue. When they reached the house the salesman could clearly see the name Barnard on the door. Once inside, the customer asked Clarence where his father was. Having been told that he was elsewhere, he sent Clarence to find him: 'This gentleman is from Tiffany's,' he said, 'and he desires the money for the goods I have purchased of them.'[12] Clarence soon returned with a cheque made out to the correct amount and signed by James W. Barnard. The salesman thanked him and left. He was only gone ten minutes when Mac and Austin left as well, in their case for good. By the time Tiffany's found out that the cheque was a useless forgery, Mac and Austin were far away. However, perhaps due to carelessness or maybe greed, they had failed to pay the accomplice who had acted as the coachman, Charles, and he gave them away to the police.[13] Mac was apprehended for the Tiffany's job while in Portland, Maine, trying to effect a 'cattle swindle'.[14] He was sentenced to two years in Sing Sing on that occasion. Austin was not found.

A few years later Mac and his brother, Michael, the proclivity for crime obviously running in the family, posed as merchants and tried to rob $500 from the Hide and Leather Bank of Boston by presenting a forged cheque. On that occasion the staff rumbled them just in time and the brothers had to flee.[15] A few months later Michael Macdonnell, along with 'a young man named Hill', was known to have used a forged cheque to defraud $2,200 from a bank in Worcester, Massachusetts.[16] They also stole a horse and wagon to make good their escape. No doubt Mac was also involved in these escapades as well.

Another attempted fraud with which Mac was definitely involved was committed around 1871 when he almost got away with $142,000 from Jay Cooke, McCulloch and Co. in New York, but in the end was discovered and had to run away empty-handed.[17] Then, in December of the same year, he arrived in Louisville, Kentucky and, under the name of 'Sweet', initiated a so-called 'check-raising' scheme, a fraud based on forged cheques.[18] Although they didn't know it, by this time Mac and his colleagues were under observation by two detectives, Bligh and Gallagher, with the result that they were arrested.[19] When Mac's possessions were searched by the police, items which can only be described as tools of the professional forger's trade were found, such as official letterheads and envelopes from a number of banks, various inks, pens and erasers, a stamp with the initials G.M. on it, and a cheque book and cheques from Baxter, Bell and Co., a large firm of cotton factors in New Orleans.[20] Two letters were also discovered: one from a firm of bankers in Louisville called John Schmidt and Co. and another from a bank in Nashville. The police were intrigued by the fact that the forgers had managed, by some chemical means, to erase all the writing between the date and the signature on both of these letters.[21] The documents were all ready for some imaginative new text to be inserted. Mac was in custody for only a week when some influential friends in New York arranged for a law firm in Louisville to get him out on a bond of $1,000. The money was subsequently forfeited when Mac absconded to New York.

Mac was another person, just like George Bidwell, who had come under the influence of the criminal Mr Kibbe. According to George, Mac also ended up being swindled by Kibbe.[22] It seems that it was during one of his periods of incarceration that Mac first got to know George Bidwell. Mac was a cellmate of a friend that George was arranging to have released from gaol by means of bribery, and George was kind enough to arrange Mac's release as well. No doubt he soon recognized that Mac's abilities would make him a valuable criminal associate. Mac went on to become a close friend of the Bidwells and he was their first choice for this latest trip to Europe. George would have been well aware that Mac's level of sophistication and education would be ideal when they were trying to pass themselves off as rich, respectable American businessmen in Europe.

The fourth member of the gang travelling to Europe in 1872 was George Engles, otherwise known as Gottlieb Engles. Engles was named by the *The New York Times* as 'the most accomplished forger in the country'.[23] He was more generally known as 'The Terror of Wall Street'.[24] George described the German national as 'blue-eyed, blond-haired', 'slim in stature', 'well educated' and 'a good business man'.[25] His weaknesses were that he was an excessive drinker and gambler to the extent that, according to George, 'although the product of his numerous forgeries amounted in the aggregate to hundreds of thousands, he never had any money long.' His relationship with George Bidwell would soon prove to be a tempestuous one.

What specifically inspired this small but seasoned group of professional criminals to travel to Europe in the first place is interesting to consider. Perhaps it was simply that with their list of crimes growing in America and their methods and faces becoming ever more familiar to the police there, the Bidwells felt it had grown too hot for them at home and it was an opportune time to go away for a while and try their hand somewhere else. The authorities in the United States had intelligence that a group of very serious fraudsters were planning something big at the beginning of the 1870s. Some thought that it was about to happen on home soil:

Deposits in small amount were to be made in different banks, and certificated checks to be obtained thereon, which were to be altered, and, by simultaneous action, the forgers expected to make a haul amounting in the aggregate to hundreds of thousands of dollars.[26]

Perhaps the Bidwells were a party to this and something went wrong with the plan and they decided to switch their focus to Europe instead. Others believed that Europe had been the target all along. Detective Pinkerton, for instance, was one of those who had heard that a well-financed plan was afoot to take the skills of some of the best American fraudsters abroad:

> The original subscribers to the capital necessary [to carry out the Great Fraud on the Bank of England] are stated by Detective Pinkerton to have been Walter Sheridan, George Wilkes, Andrew J. Roberts and Frank Gleason.[27]

According to this theory, the Great Fraud on the Bank of England was originally part of a well-financed and highly organized criminal operation backed by important villains in America. Many believed that a disagreement then arose between the parties involved and the plan fell apart. Pinkerton related a story in which two of the backers went to England and were not pleased with the behaviour they saw exhibited there by the Bidwells and Mac. They were, so the story went, found to be 'associating with disreputable women in the Argyle and Barnes in London'.[28] This version of events, however, poses the question of whether it is credible to believe that behaviour of this type would so upset the criminal backers of the scam that they 'at once withdrew their capital' and went home. According to this story, it was Walter Sheridan who was originally supposed to be the fourth member of the gang in London, but after his visit there George Engles took his place instead.[29]

Whether or not the trip to Europe was initiated as part of a big international operation with important backers made little difference in the end to those at the operational end of the scheme. This small gang led by the Bidwells was ready and able to go ahead alone and they were about to initiate one of the greatest frauds that London had ever seen.

CHAPTER 9

England

By April 1872 they were in England. George had taken lodgings with Engles at the house of Mrs Ann Thomas, 21 Enfield
Road, Haggerstone, London, and told his new landlady that his
name was Mr Anthony. His friend, whom she described as 'the
fair gentleman', was called Mr Swift. Although Mrs Thomas only
asked for rent of 15s. a week, George agreed to give her £1 a
week on the basis that they could leave at any time without giving
notice. Rather wisely, he had his eye on the quick getaway. He
was always careful to exude charm and politeness to those he met
and Mrs Thomas, like all the other landlords and landladies, had
no complaints to make about her American lodgers. She found
them to be very agreeable and took them to be 'rich gentlemen on
tour'.[1] Mac and Austin found lodgings elsewhere in London, for
a time at the Grosvenor Hotel, and all four of them met daily at
Enfield Road.

George moved out of Mrs Thomas's house on 22 April 1872,
and on 29 April Engles paid up whatever they owed her and left as
well. As it happened George had forgotten to return his latch key
to Mrs Thomas and so he posted it to her along with a gracious
letter thanking her for her 'attention'.[2] That letter was addressed
from the Terminus Hotel, London Bridge. Austin also called once
to Mrs Thomas's house to collect a few things that his friends had
left behind, including two hats, a bottle of hair restorer and a
number of shirt studs.

They may have seemed like gentlemen, but the truth was that as
soon as they had arrived in Europe the Americans had got busy
straightaway with their criminal activities. They began travelling

around various cities in Europe engaging in the scam that had by now become their speciality, i.e. the passing of fake financial documents in return for cash. Apart from England, their 'work' took them to France, Germany, the Netherlands and Belgium. Their favourite jobs tended to be those that could be executed quickly and with little risk. On this trip, however, they became determined to pull off something a little bigger. At some point they identified a very welcome vulnerability in the banking system in England. George was on the Continent when he received an intriguing dispatch from Mac in London:

> To George Bidwell, Amsterdam:
> Have made a great discovery. Come immediately.
> Mac.[3]

The story goes that Mac had gone to Barings Bank in London one day to get a genuine bill of exchange discounted. His experience at American banks was that when you presented one of these bills, they would send it away for validation before any payment was made. Much to his surprise, in London they just took his bill and gave him the money straightaway with no questions asked. He was amazed that it was common practice among the banks in England to pay out on bills of exchange without checking their authenticity. A criminal opportunity too good to pass up on had just presented itself.

The others were intrigued by this information. If what Mac had told them was correct and such lax scrutiny was routine, it would be quite easy for anyone to walk into a bank with a forged bill of exchange, receive payment on it, and then flee the country with the loot. It would be a quick scam, with very little risk of arrest. The forgery would not be discovered by the bank until they attempted to redeem the full value of the bill on maturity, a few months later. Yet, as they considered the matter further, they realized that to do this just once or twice would display a terrible lack of criminal ambition and so they set about planning an elaborate scheme by which they could defraud a London bank of a vast amount of money.

Their financial institution of choice became the Bank of England. Mac, in particular, thought the place was rife for such a job: 'The whole directorate of the fossil institution,' he said, 'was permeated with the dry rot of centuries.' Those in charge, he believed, 'were convinced that their banking system was impregnable, and, as a consequence ... would fall an easy victim ...'[4] Austin agreed with these sentiments:

> ... any system of finance unchanged in detail for a century, belief in the perfection of which was an article of faith not alone with the officials charged with its management, but with the people of England at large, must, in the very nature of the case, lie wide open to the attack of any man bold enough ...[5]

Having focused upon the Bank of England as their main target, Austin took on the job of opening an account there. In order to engender the correct image at the bank, he decided that, as it was such a traditional institution, it was important to be introduced by someone well known and respected there. With that in mind, he positioned himself outside the branch at Burlington Gardens one day on the lookout for suitable customers as they emerged. He followed several people back to their places of business and narrowed his search down to three individuals about whom he did some extra research, before finally settling on one person. The chosen person was the tailor, Mr Green, of Savile Row. The more he investigated Mr Green and his business, the happier he grew with his choice:

> Certainly I had hit well, for the firm (fathers and sons) had been depositors in the Bank of England for near a century, and had considerable wealth ...[6]

The challenge of creating a fictitious character who seemed rich and above suspicion was the next step for the suave Austin. He introduced himself at Green's shop as a stereotypical rich American, even down to the large cigar protruding from his mouth. With all the skill of a character actor, he became Mr Frederick Albert Warren, with a temporary address at 21 Enfield Road, Haggerstone, and, later, the Golden Cross Hotel.[7] A room was booked at the Golden Cross Hotel in the name of Mr Warren and held for a year, although no one stayed here. Even after he had been introduced at the bank by Mr Green and had opened his account, Austin was aware that every performance he gave as Warren would have to be convincing:

> A look, a word too much, a shadow, or a smile in my face might ruin all.[8]

Meanwhile George was engaged in other vital activities. He went on a trip to France, during which he conducted a flurry of successful fraudulent transactions. He sent the proceeds of his criminal activities, in the form of gold and French currency, to London by mail. It was Engles' job to collect these packages on a daily basis as they arrived at the pre-arranged address: the Queen's Hotel. Either out of fear of capture or just pure incompetence, Engles failed to do so. George's opinion on the matter was that Engles was a coward. He was, George said, one who always left the risks 'to the more foolhardy'.[9] This left George, on his return to London, with the problem of having to pick up the loot himself in bulk:

> I immediately took a valuable hand-bag filled with linen, etc., went direct to the hotel, registered the name to which I had addressed the letters, asked if there were any letters for me, and they were all handed over forthwith.[10]

Since Engles had failed to do his part in the job, George now called upon him to travel to Paris with the gold and paper money in order to get it changed. Engles did agree to go, but then George found out that he had taken an assistant to Paris with him, whom he got to do most of the dangerous work.

A trip to South America was planned, probably to raise money for the European trip and in order to get sample bills of exchange that could be copied for use in the fraud on the Bank of England. Engles prepared the forged papers that were needed but in doing so, from George's point of view, he made an error that ruined the whole trip and put the others in danger. Engles insisted on forging the fake letters of credit with only one signature, that of the bank manager, whereas George wanted him to include the signature of both the bank manager and the sub-manager. In Engles' opinion, that was unnecessary. It led to yet another acrimonious dispute between the two, but as Engles was an expert in the forgery of documents, George allowed his opinion to prevail. That was a mistake.

Relations between George and Engles had become soured to such an extent by then that, once the papers were prepared, Engles abandoned the whole European trip and went back to the United States. On 28 May 1872, George, Austin and Mac travelled to Rio in South America on board the *Lusitania*.[11] The existence of only one signature on the letters made the bank officials in Rio suspicious and, in the end, George and the others had to flee the continent. One has to wonder if Engles ever wanted them to succeed. George was, understandably, furious about the whole episode:

> In yielding to him the point ... as to whether both the manager's and sub-manager's names should appear on the forged letters of credit, I acquiesced in a step which virtually defeated the whole scheme, and changed an easy money-making affair into what just missed turning out a tragedy.[12]

Back in London in August 1872, Mac and Austin moved into lodgings on the drawing-room floor of a house owned by Mrs Ellen Rose Green at 1 Langham Street. Their landlady noticed that 'they used to be away for some days at a time'.[13] She also knew that a man called George Bidwell often called to see them. Both she and her son noticed Mac's impressive walking stick, which 'was gold-headed with diamonds'.[14]

George took a room at Nelson's Hotel in Great Portland Street and, as usual, became friendly with the manager there, Kate Mary English. He told her that he had been staying at another hotel with his brother, but that he preferred her place as it was 'smaller and more quiet'.[15] She also got to know Austin and Mac, who called to see George frequently. Kate Mary noticed that George travelled a lot during this time, going to Eastbourne for a week and on a number of trips to the Continent. He asked if Kate Mary would be willing to receive some letters for him while he was away from London and forward them on to him, which she agreed to do. After some time she received correspondence from him asking her to send any letters that had arrived to the Grand Hotel St James, in Paris.[16] Then she received another letter from him, dated Saturday 14 September, saying that he was by then at the Grand Hotel de Paris in Trouville:

> In case you have any letters for me on receipt of this, will you please forward them to this hotel, but not afterwards, as I expect to leave here shortly, and shall let you know where to send them?[17]

He sent another letter from Paris, dated 20 September, and yet another dated 22 October from the Hotel de l'Europe, Hamburg, in which he gave another forwarding address at the Hotel d'Angleterre, Frankfurt.[18] A number of letters had arrived for him from America and Kate Mary posted them on to Frankfurt.

After some time Mac arrived at the hotel, paid Kate Mary English the outstanding postage and said that Mr Bidwell was most obliged to her for taking the trouble to send on the letters. He told her that George had received them all. From then on, Mac told her, he would be calling to collect the letters for Mr Bidwell, which he did.

During their travels on the Continent, Mac succumbed to a bout of illness, the symptoms of which resembled malaria. George then came down with the same condition, which laid him low for a week. Mac was taking time to recover his health, but the Bidwell brothers did not panic about the planning of the Great Fraud on the Bank of England. Austin sent Mac a considerate letter on 5 October:

> ... the first consideration is your health, and if necessary we will postpone business until Christmas, and, if you require rest for ten days or more, for Heaven's sake take it; it might be highly dangerous for you to stir about. Then we have a good capital, and, when ready, can largely increase it on short order. Above all things, if your health requires it, let us wait, for

business cannot be injured by delay; it is only a matter of resting for that time.[19]

Illness was not the only obstacle; a trip to Holland proved somewhat problematic for George as well. He had difficulty in getting any of his frauds to work over there. 'We never transact business of any kind with persons unknown to us' was the answer he received most often to his inquiries.[20] In frustration, he decided to employ a different method. He had some genuine bills of exchange in his possession drawn on merchants in Amsterdam, which he had bought in Frankfurt on an earlier trip. He decided to use these to achieve some credibility in the financial community over there. He visited the merchants who had issued the bills and, telling them that he needed money, asked if they would be willing to pay out on them early, minus a discount. They all informed him that it was their practice only to pay out on bills that were due, which was the answer he expected. The interaction did allow him, however, to get from them the contact details of a number of brokers who might be willing to discount the bills for him.

One name given to him was that of a broker called Mr Pinto. George called on Mr Pinto, telling him that he had been given his name by a merchant with whom he did business. Pinto found the recommendation from the merchant a sufficient reference, and agreed to do business with George.[21] These transactions provided George with documents that proved very useful in the fraud at the Bank of England.

CHAPTER 10

Preparation, Groundwork and the Arrival of Noyes

The planning for the Great Fraud on the Bank of England had to be meticulous. The forged bills of exchange would have to look just like genuine ones. The plan relied on the hope that the Bank of England would simply credit their account without carrying out any checks of validity on the forged bills of exchange. That money would then be withdrawn from Mr Warren's account and deposited into another bank account, from where, in turn, it would be moved on further. It would, ultimately, be shipped back to America in some form such as American bonds, jewellery or gold. The Americans would carry out this fraud repeatedly until the first bills became due for full payment, and then be safely across the Atlantic, enjoying the proceeds of the crime, before the alarm could be raised.

Once they returned from the failed trip to South America, they began to deposit whatever funds they could into the account of Mr F.A. Warren at the Bank of England, so that 'the large balance would show well on the bank's books'.[1] Meanwhile, Austin, as Mr Warren, was engaged in charming Colonel Francis and his staff, impressing them with the progress of his business enterprise and lulling them into the false sense of security upon which much of the later deception would depend. It was essential that the staff at the Burlington Gardens branch harboured no suspicions about him when the fake bills started to arrive at the bank.

The institution chosen for the second account, which would be essential in order to launder the illegal money, was the Continental

Bank on Lombard Street. Once again Austin was called upon to use his powers of impersonation. This time he took on the role of playing Mr Charles Johnson Horton, in whose name he opened the account on 2 December 1872. Apart from moving their personal lodgings frequently and keeping the room at the Golden Cross Hotel, they had also rented a number of other rooms for their purpose. Room number six at the Terminus Hotel, London Bridge, was taken by Mr C.J. Horton. He told the proprietor, Mr Albert Gearing, that 'he might require it for two or three days, or possibly two or three weeks, as an office, until he could obtain suitable accommodation in the city'.[2] Mr Gearing first let Mr Horton into the room on 11 January, at a rate of 6s. a day. After that he only saw him once or twice. He told Mr Gearing that his clerk would attend the room 'daily on business'.[3]

Another room was booked at the Cannon Street Hotel. Room number eight was taken there on 30 January 1872. Peter Steinmayer was a waiter there and he later thought the name of the man who booked the room was Horton. Mr Horton was a bit of a mystery though. Steinmayer did not know where the man came from or why he even wanted the room: 'He used to come to the hotel about three or four times a week, and stay about twenty minutes or half an hour. Two or three gentlemen called there to see him.'[4]

With Engles' abrupt departure, the gang was left a man down. Another person was required in order to carry out the scam effectively and safely, and this is how Noyes, full name Edwin Noyes Hills, first got involved in the scam. George began trying to contact him as soon as Engles had left England, with the aim of getting him to come to London as soon as possible. In a letter that he sent to Kate Mary English at Nelson's Hotel, dated 14 September 1872, from the Grand Hotel de Paris, Trouville, he wrote:

> I have addressed a letter to Mr. Edwin Hills, and should he arrive please hand it to him when he asks for it.... . Of course, if my brother calls you may hand any letters or other things to him or to my other friend; but the letter enclosed for Mr. Hills you may please say nothing of to them, merely holding it for the personal call of Mr. Hills, either Edwin or E. N. Hills.[5]

In another letter dated 22 October 1872, sent from the Hotel de l'Europe, Hamburg, George again asked Kate Mary English whether Mr Hills had called, but he had not.[6] When Mac began collecting George's mail from Nelson's Hotel, Kate Mary English asked him what she should do about the letter for Mr Hills. He told her that he knew nothing about it and that she had better do with it what Mr Bidwell had said. As Mr Hills did not arrive, Kate Mary English sent the letter back to George. When George arrived back in London he again asked Kate Mary whether Mr Hills had called. When she told him that he had not, George left another letter for him and asked her to give it to him when he did arrive. On the same day that Austin opened the Horton account, George sent a telegram to Noyes in New York, telling him to join them in London immediately:

Come Wednesday steamer without fail ...[7]

Known to the others as 'Noyes', Edwin Noyes Hills was twenty-eight years of age at the time and was a long-time criminal associate of the Bidwells and Mac. Born in Hartford, Connecticut, to decent farming people, Noyes, as he put it himself, soon 'began to look about ... for something better than farm work'.[8] His desire to succeed in life led him first to Wall Street but, unfortunately, the 'something better' in his life soon turned out to be crime, and most particularly the crime of fraud. This brought him to the Bidwell brothers, of whom the young farm boy became a great admirer. He described them as 'accomplished men. Well read and of most charming manners – qualities which carried them through many a tight place.'[9] Noyes had been arrested in New Jersey and sentenced to seven years in state prison for a job he did with those other criminal brothers, the Macdonnells, at the bank in Sturtevant. He had only just been released in 1872 when he was invited by George to come and do this work in London.[10]

Noyes managed to get on board the White Star steamship *Atlantic* when it sailed out of New York for Liverpool on 7 December 1872.[11] The voyage cost him $80 and he 'occupied a separate cabin during a portion of the time'.[12] He was the only 'Mr Hills' on board that voyage and did not try very hard to keep a low profile. He was introduced to the purser, Mr William Guest Barrett, in New York, by Mr Law who was a 'clerk to Mr Sparks, the owners' agent in that city'.[13] It was obvious to Mr Barrett, from the 'several conversations' he had with Mr Hills, that he was an American.[14] Noyes also became acquainted with James Erving, the saloon steward on board the *Atlantic*.

Noyes arrived in England on 17 December 1872 without, it seems, bringing any luggage. Kate Mary English, at Nelson's Hotel, finally got to meet the mysterious Mr Hills when he turned up there looking for a letter. When she asked him if he was Mr Bidwell's friend, he said that he was:

> She remarked that she had been expecting him for a long time, and she gave him the letter which Bidwell had left. He read it, and then asked her to be kind enough to take in any letters which might come for him, adding that he had first intended to stop at the hotel, but he had altered his plans and was going to live with a friend a little way out of London. She agreed to receive the letters, and he called a fortnight afterwards and took away those which had been delivered.[15]

Noyes was immediately impressed by the lifestyles that were being led by his friends, the Bidwells and Mac, in London:

> I came over and found them living in luxury, and apparently in command of enormous sums of money ... They moved in the very best society, and were everywhere accepted as distinguished and wealthy Americans.[16]

Noyes was told that his chief duty in this job would be the operation of the account held in the name of Mr C.J. Horton at the Continental Bank and so the others began preparing him for that role at once. On the 18 and 19 December their preoccupation was with dressing him in a manner that was suitable for his role as Mr Horton's clerk. One of the places to which they brought him was Messrs Kino, a firm of tailors on Regent Street, where the salesman, Henry T. Hagger, fitted him out in suitable attire. Noyes gave a false name and his address as Nelson's Hotel in Great Portland Street.[17]

Then they also set about establishing his *bona fides* by placing that advertisement in the *Daily Telegraph*, from 6 to 11 January, in the guise of someone looking for a position as a clerk. Noyes made sure to show that advertisement to a number of people at Durrants Hotel, where he was staying, telling them that he had placed it. Many genuine responses were received by post at the hotel. Noyes then held a very conspicuous meeting with a gentleman whom he told everyone was 'Mr Charles Horton' regarding, he let it be known, the recent advertisement. On this occasion the role of Mr Horton was played by Mac instead of Austin. Some days later, Noyes told everyone that he had been appointed to the position of Mr Horton's clerk and 'had deposited 300*l*. with him as a guarantee for his good conduct'.[18] His story was so convincing that James Richardson, the waiter, tried to warn him off the idea of trusting anyone in London with £300.

They even arranged for the legal document to be drawn up by the solicitor, Mr Howell in Cheapside, laying out the terms of the contractual agreement between Mr Horton and his clerk. This farcical agreement, entered into on 11 January 1873, cost them £10 in legal fees but they felt that it was worth it to make everything look legitimate in case Noyes needed to back up his story.

Noyes was then introduced at the Continental Bank as Mr Horton's clerk and it was made clear to the staff there that he was legally empowered to conduct all of his employer's financial transactions in Mr Horton's absence. The beauty of this elaborate subterfuge was supposed to be that if the fraud should ever be discovered, all Noyes would have to do was claim that he was merely an employee of the mysterious businessman, Mr Horton, and knew nothing about any fraud. George even prepared a letter for Noyes to carry on his person, which purported to show that he was engaged in carrying out the instructions of his employer and nothing more:

Dear Sir,
I shall be unable to come to the office tomorrow, as I shall be very busy at the West End, and will not be able to come as far as London Bridge. So you can go on with the business just as I told you, and don't fail to collect the money and bring it with

you to Broad Street Station at 3 o'clock, and meet me in the first class waiting room, or down at the ticket office at the foot of the stairs. I will then give you further instructions.

I am, yours, &c.,

C. J. Horton'[19]

George gave Noyes explicit instructions:

I told him he must ask no more questions, but follow my directions implicitly and promptly; that I should not even let him know where the rest of us lodged, after the first of January. I further informed him that he was to act as clerk for 'Horton', and though our operations were a little irregular, that he should be taken care of, kept out of danger, and be well paid for his services ...[20]

Mr Gearing, proprietor of the Terminus Hotel, saw Noyes at the hotel for the first time on 28 January 1873. He assumed that he was the clerk of whom Mr Horton had spoken when he booked the room. Noyes went there nearly every morning. George Cooper, a waiter at the hotel, noticed that Noyes would usually 'remain about half an hour', but he did not know what his business was. Mr Horton had paid for the room at first, but after that Noyes began to do it. Mr Gearing did notice something strange, though: 'Except writing materials he saw no signs of business going on.'[21]

Noyes' payment for the Bank of England job was to be 'about five per cent of the proceeds'. His exposure to the risk of serious custodial punishment was deemed to be far less than the others. One of his more contradictory actions during his time in London was his regular attendance at services held in Westminster Abbey on Sundays.[22] Whether this was a genuine act of religion on his behalf or a ruse to convince people of his good character is hard to tell.

CHAPTER 11

Paperwork

---·•·---

The purchase of genuine bills of exchange and other financial documents was an essential part of the scam, not only to use as models to copy, but also to establish a good credit record for Mr Warren at the Bank of England. With this in mind, on 6 December 1872, Mac called at the firm of American merchants, Messrs Richardson, Spence and Co. at 17 Water Street in Liverpool. He asked one of the clerks there, Mr William Anderson, if they had any first-class banker's bills for sale, saying that he had received a large sum of money. He claimed to have seen their name on letters of credit. Although Anderson told him that he was more likely to get what he wanted in London, he had one of his colleagues, Mr Coupland, show him the way to Messrs Edward W. Yates and Co. who were bankers at 37 Castle Street in Liverpool. They might, he said, be able to help.

Mac was dealt with at Yates and Co. by Mr Edward Yates himself. He told Mr Yates that his firm had been recommended to him by Messrs Richardson, Spence and Co. and that he had £1,000 or £2,000 'which he wished to invest for a month for two' and was looking for banker's bills to buy.[1] He was, he told Mr Yates, travelling from America to London. Mr Yates showed him a number of banker's bills that he had at that time and Mac selected one for £1,000, which he bought less a discount of £11 6s.[2] He returned a few days later to purchase another bill, but this time Mr Yates told him that he had 'none to sell'.[3]

Information on what were the best and most solvent firms in Europe was also important and with that in mind, while on their travels the fraudsters gathered whatever financial information they could:

> ... they were actively engaged in various capitals and cities of Europe in making inquiries as to the solvency and status of the various large commercial houses, and the amount of respect their bills were likely to command in London, and in acquainting themselves generally with the ordinary course of trading transactions there and in this country, so that they might be perfectly armed at every step of their way.[4]

As for the forged documents themselves, they knew as experienced forgers that any fake bills of exchange passed on to the Bank of England would have to look like authentic documents. They would have to appear as if they had actually been issued by, or on behalf of, reputable companies and banks throughout Europe. Consequently, George set about amassing a collection of inks in a wide variety of colours. He also managed to get examples of the endorsements, the stamps and the signatures used by many of Europe's leading firms.

They were also well aware that, if the documents were to look authentic, they would require professional expertise and equipment. They would need good-quality documents printed not only in English, but also in French, German, Dutch, Russian, Turkish and Arabic. They also required good wood engravings to replicate the stamps used by a number of banks and other companies. George sent Mac to Paris to see if they could source what they needed over there. Mac returned empty-handed, claiming that he could not get them and that there were no decent engravers in that city. George was annoyed, later, when he found out that Mac had 'whiled away the time, and returned to play that tale on my credulity'.[5] George resolved to take care of it himself. He did considerable research into the tradesmen of London, including the use of the City Directory that the police would later find at Mac's lodgings, before finally selecting a number of tradesmen to undertake various aspects of the job.

The criminals even had the audacity to order two books of blank bills of exchange from the printing and stationery company owned by the family of the Lord Mayor of London himself, Sir Sydney Waterlow. On 4 December 1872, a man calling himself Mr Warren called on Mr Thomas Lyell, a clerk at Messrs Waterlow and Son in Birchin Lane, and asked to choose 'some patterns of bills of exchange'.[6] The man chose two patterns from those shown to him, but requested that 'an oval picture at the top of them might be omitted in each, and also the name Waterlow and Co.'[7] He was told that first of all a sketch would be drawn up for his approval and after that he could decide on the colours to be used. In the end, he settled on two forms using 'various coloured inks'.[8] He ordered 500 copies, 250 of each type and, in lieu of providing a reference, agreed to pay a deposit in advance of £2. The address he gave was the Cannon Street Hotel. He called a number of times and, on one occasion, was dealt with by Mr Lyell's colleague, James Mowatt. Mr Warren's order was finally ready for him on 17 December and he called to collect it himself. He was satisfied with the results, but said that he wanted to take away the plates from which the bills had been printed. This was unusual, but they sent him to their office, which was located at London Wall where the objects were kept, 'with a request that the plates might be delivered to him'.[9]

From 9 December 1872 until the end of February 1873 George called many times to the business premises of Nelson and Co. based at Oxford Arms Passage, Warwick Lane. He was attended to by Mr George Boole Challoner, who knew him by the name Mr J.R. Nelson. George placed an order for 'a small electro plate' with the type set up to print words in German. He provided an exact example on card of the words that he wanted to use and the form required.[10] Challoner charged him 2s. for the plate and Bidwell collected it a day or two later:

It was a mounted electro-plate screwed or pinned on a block of wood, and ... without a handle.[11]

On other occasions he purchased from Mr Boole Challoner bills of exchange and 'some printing ink and a piece of brass rule, on which lines were generally printed'.[12] He never gave any specific address, but did mention Brighton 'as a place near where he was staying'.[13] On one visit he mentioned needing the services of a lithographer and Boole Challoner gave him the name of Mr Straker at 16 Ivy Lane.

Around 18 or 19 December 1872, George called to see Mr Thomas Straker. At first he did not give Straker any name, but 'after he had been several times' he gave him the name Mr Brooks.[14] He told Mr Straker that he had been recommended to him by Messrs Nelson and Co. as someone 'who did work on copper-plate'.[15] He had two copper plates with him to which he wanted various changes made. He also needed 500 copies made. He asked what price Straker could do them for and the printer replied that he could do them for 15s., which was the trade price, but they would not be ready before Christmas. George told him that he would pay 5s. extra if he could get them done before Christmas and Straker said that he would try. As it happened, some of the order was completed by Christmas Eve and, although Mr Straker was not at his place of work that day, the order was delivered. Straker believed that Mr Brooks was in the printing trade and that he was 'getting up the bills as samples for different firms'.[16] At no time was he suspicious of Mr Brooks or the order that he had placed. Mr Brooks was concerned about the impression that would be left on the copper plates after a printing job: he asked Straker about this and was told that they were rubbed off with 'a snake stone' once the job was finished. They showed him how it was done. Straker assured him that it 'entirely obliterated the work' and agreed that 'after the impression had been obliterated ... he could not print any more from it if he were to give him 100*l*'.[17] This seemed to satisfy Mr Brooks.

George also transacted business with a deaf engraver and wood-cutter called Mr James Dalton, who had a business premises at 26 Paternoster Row. He first met with Mr Dalton near the end of November 1872, and 'did business with him from time to time' until 22 February 1873.[18] As George got Dalton to produce some wooden blocks with German writing on them, the wood engraver just presumed him to be a German. He even referred to him in his account books by the word 'Herr'.[19] During that period George called frequently, on occasion up to 'four times a day'. Unlike the other tradesmen, however, Dalton did find him suspicious. He disliked the way he would arrive frequently at his premises, grab the blocks, pay his money and then leave without looking for a receipt. Dalton later claimed that at one point he had even written a letter to the magistrate, Sir Thomas Henry, outlining his suspicions about his customer, but his relatives had persuaded him to destroy it.[20]

Mr William Cheshire, an engraver based in Paternoster Row, was another who did work for George. Mr Cheshire did not know his name and, in fact, also took him to be a German.[21] Mr Cheshire cut some blocks for him with the words: 'Berlin, Hamburg, Lubeck, Bremen and Amsterdam.'[22] He also made a number of stamps for him. All in all, George was pleased with the results that he got from the tradesmen of London.

CHAPTER 12

Dear Daisy and Almost Tragedy on a French Train

W̲hile living in England, Austin's attention had not been completely taken up with fraudulent financial matters. He had become involved with a young lady called Frances Catherine Grey from Pimlico. He first met Frances, or Daisy as he affectionately called her, at her place of employment, a drinking establishment called the Turkish Divan in Haymarket, where she was a barmaid. Austin had a fascination with English barmaids:

> Barmaids are a great institution in England – that is, they never have more than one man behind a bar, none at all in the railway bars … These girls are chosen for their beauty and attractiveness … How easily and how naturally, too, does a young man become ensnared.[1]

The Turkish Divan was a popular place to socialize for Americans staying in London. Daisy knew Austin as Theodore Bingham and began calling him 'Dory' for short.[2] She also got to know Mac and Noyes at the Turkish Divan. She was aware that they were all Americans, and they told her that Mac was Austin's doctor and Noyes was 'a genius who had come over [to England] to invent something'.[3] The three Americans became regular customers and usually arrived together, although Daisy noticed that Noyes remained very quiet and 'generally sat apart from the others'.[4] It did not take long for her to fall for the exotic American charm of Austin and a relationship blossomed between them.

Daisy bade her American lover goodbye at Charing Cross Station in January 1873 as he set off on a short 'business' trip to Paris. It was to be a routine visit of two or three days, the purpose of which was to buy a bill of exchange from the prestigious bank owned by Messrs Rothschild. In the end, however, it turned out to be a very eventful trip: Austin was on board an express train heading for Paris when it became derailed and crashed. The incident was serious enough for three people to be killed. Although he was injured and taken away from the scene on a stretcher, Austin survived. It was, of course, a traumatic experience: 'I had fallen into a sound sleep before the train started,' he wrote later, 'and was aroused from it to find myself hurled about the compartment ...'.[5]

Austin had, according to Mac, 'as narrow an escape from instant death and being smashed to pieces as any man ever had'.[6] The intriguing thing is that the ever-resourceful American fraudster managed to turn even this horrific experience to his advantage. Once recovered sufficiently, but hardly able to walk, he headed straight for his destination, Rothschild's, one of the most powerful banking houses in the world. Alphonse de Rothschild was not only head of their bank in Paris but also, as it happened, a director of the railway company on which Austin had been injured.[7] Austin hobbled into the bank with the aid of a walking stick and sporting a bandage on his head. Once he had made it known that he was one of the victims of the recent train accident, it was not long before he was speaking to the baron in person:

> ... a slight, sallow man of about 43 appeared, wearing an old-fashioned stovepipe hat and a shabby suit of snuff-coloured garments. The look of the attendants testified that the deity was before me ...[8]

Having offered his abject apologies for what had happened, the baron offered Austin the use of his personal physician or anything else that he needed. Austin told him that no more apologies were required and that he did not require a physician. Perhaps, however, the baron would help him by allowing him to use the services of his fine bank to transmit his money safely back to London. The baron, of course, said that this would be no trouble at all and he told the manager to facilitate the injured American in any way that he could. What Austin wanted was a three-month bill of exchange drawn on their London house for £4,500, the amount that he had in his possession.

Austin paid the money and sometime later the bill was delivered to his hotel.[9] Austin knew that this document would not only look impressive to the bank officials in London when he paid it into Mr Warren's account, but it would also give the gang a genuine Rothschild's bill of exchange from which to make fake copies.

When Austin returned to London, Daisy was shocked by his condition: his face was bandaged and he was just about able to walk.[10] When Mac saw him, he was also extremely concerned about his friend's health:

> ... he was in such a condition that it was almost impossible for him to move. He was helped from the station to the hotel where I was then stopping.[11]

Mac sent for Dr Coulson who, having examined him, said that Austin 'was in very great danger of being paralyzed for life, that his spine was affected'.[12] Nevertheless, no matter how much he was suffering, on 17 January Austin was able to get to the Bank of England and place that impressive genuine bill of exchange from Rothschild's on Colonel Francis's desk. Even in his weakened condition, he endeavoured to make as much fuss of the bill as he could. Of course no one at the bank knew it but Mac had practically carried him as far as the entrance door and was waiting outside to help him back to bed at the hotel afterwards. Although Austin told Colonel Francis and Mr Fenwick that business interests were calling him back to Birmingham and that he would not be back at the bank for a while, the truth was that he was about to leave the country. He would be far away when his brother George started sending in the forged bills of exchange. Neither Mr Fenwick nor Colonel Francis would ever see him at the bank again.

When Austin left England, Daisy believed that her 'Dory' was only going to the South of France for a short while to recover from his injuries. Mac later gave her a rather worrying update regarding a pistol ball that had been lodged in Austin's body:

> ... Macdonnell said he [Austin] had extracted a ball from his side after the accident. He said the ball was there before the accident, and so affected him afterwards that it became necessary to remove it.[13]

Mac delivered a number of letters to her from Austin and also passed on some money. In the last of these letters Austin told his 'dear Daisy' that he could only write with difficulty as a result of his accident and therefore would write no more for a time. In fact, although she did not know it yet, Daisy would neither see nor hear from her Dory again.

CHAPTER 13

The Beginning

Up to now all the bills of exchange that had been sent to the Bank of England for discount, including the prestigious one from Rothschild's, had been genuine. When the time came, they would all be paid out on without any difficulty. The staff at the Bank of England had no reason at all to be suspicious about the transactions taking place with regard to Mr Warren's account. All the documents that the Americans needed were now ready and Austin was out of the country. Everything was in place. George felt reasonably reassured about the feasibility of the scam:

> ... it appeared as certain as any human event that, with proper precautions and skilful handling, the scheme could be carried out without our real names becoming known, and that no clue need be left by which any trace of the perpetrators could be discovered.[1]

On 21 January 1873, the Great Fraud on the Bank of England was initiated for real when George posted that first batch of forged bills, worth £4,250, from Birmingham to London in the name of Mr F.A. Warren. George had reserved room number 18 for himself at the Queen's Hotel, Birmingham, for the purpose. Of course, once he had posted the correspondence to London, he became worried that the whole enterprise, even after all their careful preparation, could come to an abrupt end if the bills were detected as forgeries. He waited, not without considerable anxiety, to see what would happen next:

... for despite the fair look of the thing, it was difficult to believe otherwise than the bank had what looked like a vulnerable point guarded in some way that had escaped my scrutiny.[2]

As professional criminals, George and Mac had made sure that they had a quick getaway scheme prepared in the event of the fraud being discovered. They had withdrawn most of their money from the banks in London, apart from £100. George waited alone in Birmingham and it was with great trepidation that he went to the post office the following day to collect the mail addressed to Mr F.A. Warren. He realized that as soon as he asked for it, the police might swoop and arrest him. To his great relief, nothing happened. He was handed one letter posted from London. As he read it he was relieved to see that the reply from Colonel Francis was routine yet very friendly. He even asked after Mr Warren's health.

George knew then that they had succeeded. Their first forged bills had got through the system unquestioned and the amount was now credited to Mr F.A. Warren's account. The next step was to get the money out of that account and into the one held in the name of Mr C.J. Horton at the Continental Bank. They wrote a number of cheques adding up to the value of £4,000 drawn on Mr Warren's account and Noyes then deposited those in the Horton account at the Continental Bank. To complete the process, they then used cheques from the Horton account to buy £3,000 worth of United States bonds purchased at Jay Cooke, McCulloch and Co. in Lombard Street. These would then be shipped fairly easily to America.

The *modus operandi* was now established and working. During the weeks that followed the gang proceeded to carry out the fraud in the same way. A favoured practice of George's was to have Noyes draw out the funds from the Horton account in Bank of England notes and then have these exchanged for gold. The gold was then changed back into notes by someone else. George liked the trail of confusion and disconnection that this left behind:

The object of this double exchange was to break the connection, it being obligatory that a list of the numbers of all notes paid out, and to whom, must be preserved by bankers and other dealers.[3]

They also liked to buy easily transportable items such as jewellery with the money. An essential element of the plan was getting these various assets back to America. They posted a large number of United States bonds to various addresses back home. It seems that they could not countenance sending letters with contents of that value without getting some insurance on them. On 24 February 1873, Mac called into the offices of the Royal Exchange Assurance Office and asked the underwriter, Mr Edward Francis Gedge, whether they sold insurance on registered letters to New York. Mr Gedge told him that they did and Mac proceeded to insure 'a bundle of United States bonds'.[4]

> An insurance was effected from London to New York for 2,100*l*. The bonds would go in a registered letter. The price for the insurance was 3*l*. 5*s*. 1*d*. net.[5]

Mac told him that he wanted the policy in the name 'E.N. Hills, New York'. He then called out the numbers of the bonds and Mr Gedge wrote them on a slip, which Mac then signed: 'for E. N. Hills, Geo. Macdonnell.' Mac called again the next day and this time insured a letter from London to New York, containing securities of the value of £3,600. He told Mr Gedge that he wanted this one in the name of A. Biron Bidwell, New York. Once again he signed for it.[6]

While engaged in the activity of hiding the proceeds of the fraud, it was necessary for the Americans to visit various financial institutions in order to buy the bonds that they needed. It was not always that easy to get suspicious business-people in London to work with strangers from another country. On Friday 21 February 1873, Mac paid a visit to one such place, a stockbroking and sharebroking firm run by Mr James Searle and Mr Watson at Bartholomew House. He was there to price and, hopefully, buy £10,000 worth of United States bonds. Searle and Watson told him that they normally only took on new customers who brought a letter of introduction from a reputable person, and even when Mac told them he would pay in notes or gold, they were not satisfied. Mac told them that he was from South America but had been living in Paris. Eventually, he did persuade them to do business with him, but only under strict conditions. They agreed to sell him £10,000 worth of United States bonds, but he had to give a £500 Bank of England note up front, for which they gave him a receipt and a contract for the purchase of the bonds:

> They sent the 500*l*. note over to the Bank immediately after he left, and had it cashed ... not knowing the gentleman.[7]

Mac returned the following day to complete the purchase, the price coming to £10,516 including their commission.[8] Once again he paid in notes. Just as cautious as before, Searle and Watson insisted that he wait until they had sent the notes to the bank, to make sure they were genuine. Once that was done, they gave him the bonds and he signed 'Geo. Macdonnell' for them. He called again later, saying that he had more money to invest. As well as US bonds he said that he was interested in 'London joint-stock bank shares and other securities'. They told him it was too late to do any business on that particular day, but they gave him a stock exchange price list to take away and told him to call again. They were still very suspicious of doing business with someone about whom they knew so little, and Mac never returned – he must have been relieved that the Bank of England was not so cautious.

Messrs J.S. Morgan and Co., merchants of 22 Old Broad Street, was another place of business visited by Mac with the intention of hiding the illegal money. He met the clerk there, Mr Henry West, on 1 February 1873, and opened an account with them. He was able to produce 'a letter of credit from their correspondent in Paris' but they told him that it was their custom to receive a letter of introduction from all new clients.[9] Mr West agreed to open the account 'subject to their receiving a letter of introduction'.[10] Mac said that he would send to Paris immediately for such a letter. Mr West then took £1,200 from him in notes and a further £80 in gold. But then Mac returned on 20 February and, probably having thought better of the idea, said that he was leaving for America in a few days and wanted to close the account. West gave him back a cheque for £1,278 9s. 3d., which was 'the amount paid in, less the charges'.[11]

George called to the offices of Clews, Habicht and Co., bankers, at 11 Old Broad Street, London and introduced himself using the alias Mr W.J. Spaulding.[12] He did some business with them but when Alfred Lidington, the chief cashier, asked for his address, George told him that 'a letter or telegram to Brighton would find him'.[13] 'Brighton is a large place, Mr Spaulding,' Lidington said. 'You must have some address there?'[14] He did not seem to be willing to be any more forthcoming and so Lidington decided not to do any more business with him.

Noyes too had to do his best to carry out financial transactions while remaining calm and not appearing in any way suspicious as he did so. This seemed to be no problem for him. One of the places he visited was the Issues Department of the Bank of England. On 21 January 1873 he was served there by the clerk Edward Brent to whom he presented two £500 Bank of England notes, which he said he wanted exchanged for gold.[15] Mr Brent saw that on one of the notes was written: 'Noyes, 28 George Street, London'. Noyes was asked if the gold was 'for home use' or export and he replied that it was for home use. He was given the required amount of gold and left. Other visits followed, on which he was served by Mr Brent and other members of staff, and again he requested gold in exchange for notes: on 22 January, £655; on 24 January, £1,500; on 27 January, £585; on 28 January, £1,950; on 4 February, £585; on 7 February, £3,450; on 19 February, £2,800; on 21 February, £1,000;. on 25 February, £4,000; on 28 February, £2,000.[16] Some of his notes had 'E. Noyes, Durrants Hotel, Manchester Square' written on them. On some of the occasions he said that the gold was for exportation. The porters at the bank usually carried the gold to a cab for him in a black bag that he supplied himself and at no point did his activity seem to arouse suspicion.

Although doing his best not to attract any undue attention while in Birmingham, George could not help interacting with a number of people from the local community. With his unusual accent it was always possible that some of these people would remember him later. An obvious example were cab drivers. Alfred Morley, a cab proprietor from 15 Cattle Grove, Birmingham, drove him from the

Queen's Hotel to the post office on 20 February and noticed that he 'spoke with a foreign accent, something like that of a Yankee'.[17] George sent him into the post office, gave him a florin to buy a shilling stamp and told him to pick up whatever letters were there for an address that he had written on a piece of paper. Morley returned with one letter and then drove George back to his hotel. Morley saw him again about two hours later getting out of another cab at the Queen's Hotel.[18]

John Barber was another Birmingham cab driver who took George to the post office. George handed him a large stamped letter and asked him to go into the post office and register it. Mr Barber noticed that it was addressed to someone in America.[19] Afterwards he handed George the receipt and then watched him first fold it and then tear it 'into shreds' and throw it 'into the streets'.[20]

During his correspondence with Colonel Francis, George made sure he did not forget the all-important human relationship element of this scam, which had been nurtured so carefully by Austin and which reinforced significantly the trust afforded by the bank staff towards the fictitious Mr Warren. Growing increasingly confident in their continued success, the Americans found that their profit was only limited by the amount of fake bills they could generate and send to the bank. George congratulated himself that they had managed to penetrate the 'the bomb-proof vaults of the greatest financial fortress of which history gives account'.[21] Between 21 January and 28 February 1873, he sent ninety-four forged bills of exchange to the Bank of England. Understandably, George was ecstatic about the success of the scam:

> It appears as if the bank managers had heaped a mountain of gold out in the street, and had put up a notice, 'Please do not touch this,' and then had left it unguarded with the guileless confidingness of an Arcadian.[22]

The fake bills purported to come from some of the most influential institutions in the world and were forged accurately enough to fool the staff at the Bank of England into believing they were genuine. By the beginning of March 1873, to have bagged the rather staggering sum of over £102,000 was a very productive haul for any professional thief. Yet George could not entirely eliminate a sense of foreboding that was haunting him. Was it just a sense of cynicism based on years of struggle, or was it the voice of experience? On one particular evening the feeling was especially strong. The Americans were relaxing in 'a private parlour' at St James's Hotel, Piccadilly, all 'stylishly dressed' and drinking a bottle of good wine.[23] The younger members of the group were celebrating their success 'in high spirits', and, as George put it, 'saw themselves safely back in America, the possessors of fortunes, however wrongfully obtained'.[24] They could not envisage any way that the scam could go wrong now. This confidence of youth worried George. When he could endure their attitude no longer, he put his glass of wine down on the table and addressed them with a warning:

> Well, my friends, you believe that nothing can happen to hinder the full realization of your hopes, and that you are as safe as if you were already off for America; but I advise you to moderate your ardour and not be too sanguine – too certain. It is true that everything is so arranged, works so smoothly, and ourselves shrouded in so dense a fog – a London fog – of mystery, that, even in case of a premature discovery, they may not be able to reach us or get a clue to our personality...

Nevertheless, he advised them, they were not yet in the clear:

> Despite the smooth surface, I have a foreboding that Aeolus is brooding a storm that may send our gold-laden bark among the rocks, and ourselves with it. Negligence or accident will beat the 'best laid plans,' and we shall have the greatest success or the most terrible disaster possible. Let us do no more crowing until we are out of the woods.[25]

Then he left, leaving his stunned and perhaps slightly annoyed younger colleagues behind. They were in no mood for such truths.

CHAPTER 14

A Life of Luxury and Romance

---·•·---

Considering that the Americans were in the process of defrauding the Bank of England out of such a large amount of money, it is not surprising that they were living a life of luxury and enjoying the best that London had to offer. There is ample evidence to show that they were never averse to spending money on themselves. Among the items purchased by them during this time were expensive clothes from the tailors on Savile Row including silk scarves, monogrammed shirts and a hunting suit for George. A bag was purchased at Parkins & Gotto, adorned with the Bidwell coat of arms at a cost of £25. There was that fancy walking stick used by Mac with its handle crafted in the shape of a snake made from gold and its diamond eye; the one noticed by the landlady and her son in Langham Street. It had been a gift from George and Austin and was engraved: G.M. from George and Austin. George purchased a ring from Messrs Hawes & Son jewellers for £105, as well as a diamond and an expensive watch. On one visit to the diamond merchants, Welby's of Garrick Street, Austin spent £280.[1]

On 28 February 1873, Mac bought four diamonds from the diamond merchant and commission agent William Gardner for £300.[2] Mr Gardner, who was based at 5 Leith Street, Edinburgh, called on him at 17 St James's Place. Mac paid for the diamonds using three £100 bank notes.[3] Mac told him to call again later as he had a friend who might also like to buy some of his diamonds. Mr Gardner agreed to do so and met George. However, George did not buy anything from him on that occasion.

George was a very good customer of John Robert Gray, a

salesman at the jewellers Messrs Hawes. On 24 December 1872, he bought a watch from him for £5 10s.; on 29 January 1873, a ring paid for with a £100 bank note; then there was a bracelet, a brooch and some earrings which cost £52 10s. on 25 February 1873.[4]

Among the other shops frequented by the fraudsters were the 'hatters' E. Bax and Co., at 443 Strand; Newton and Co., tailors at 7 Hanover Square; Messrs Bowring and Arundel, hosiers situated in Bond Street; and Messrs Kino, tailors in Regent Street. Such was their finery, in fact, that, according to George, they were even mistaken for royalty. With George's humble beginnings, this was an event that pleased him greatly:

> During our stay in London, it was frequently remarked that Macdonnell bore a strong general resemblance to the Prince of Wales. One afternoon Mac and I were sauntering past the 'Horse-Guards,' and as soon as the magnificent sentry (placed on horseback in the gateway) saw us, he brought his sword to the salute and kept it there until we were past. Exactly who he took me for has ever since been – not a casus belli – but a subject of curious cogitations ...[5]

There were, of course, more pressing and mundane needs for the money back home in America. This was demonstrated by a letter written by Noyes to his brother Johnnie on 29 January 1873, in which he enclosed a letter of credit for £1,000 that he had got from Barings Bank on the same day:

> Dear Bro. Johnnie,
> I have this day registered a letter to you, via John W. Nixon, of Naval Office Custom House, New York City, containing 1,000l. sterling ... After you collect it, carry [$]1,400 over to Charles to pay Smith 750, and also he will pay that bond of 600, that father owes Henry Kennedy for that woodland. The bond is endorsed by John Maclean, so you will see that Kennedy will sicken of the prospect of getting a hold of our homestead... . Take 250 dollars yourself to buy your wife a 150 dollar sewing machine, a suit of nice clothes for yourself,

cotton cloth out of which Leiz. will make for herself and
mother under garments, &c, as a present from me. Don't let
Cos Jul or anyone know but that you bought them yourself.
Also deduct your and Leiz. expenses to go to Springfield and
out home. Also hand Robert Chapman 50 dollars if he should
want it (I offered to lend him it). Take a receipt for it to pay to
father when he can if I am not at home. The balance you may
place to my account in the First National Bank, Hartford,
subject to be drawn by Leiz. in case of death to me or accident
or long absence of six months. Make it draw interest. If they
will not give interest put it into the Etna Bank. Hall will introduce you. Say nothing to no one as to my whereabout, not
even Chas. I am trying to persuade a friend of mine, an English
gentleman, to go to America and enter business. If I succeed, it
will perhaps throw us together. It is not certain when I shall
return to America. These Englishmen are such sticklers for
country, it is hard to start them. I confess that I am beginning
to like to stay in Europe. More anon next time.

Yours as ever, ED[6]

Austin had enjoyed his fling with Daisy and the others made no
sacrifice on the romantic front either. In Mac's case, after Austin's
departure from London, he and Daisy became intimate. George's
particular favourite was Nelly Vernon, while Noyes had taken up
with Ellen Franklin. All of these women would later become
central to the police investigation.

George had first met Nelly Vernon in August 1872 when she
was living at 11 Duke's Road. They began to see each other for
dinner every day and he introduced her to the best in high life that
London had to offer. Although George was much older than the
twenty-year-old Nelly, before long an intimate relationship developed between them. One night, at the beginning of September
1872, he took her to the Covent Garden Theatre, where they
enjoyed a private box. There she met Austin for the first time, who
George told her was his brother, and Mac, who he said was a
friend.[7]

Later that month Nelly accompanied George on a trip to
France, where they spent time in Trouville. Unfortunately, Nelly

became ill and had to return home to London for a while before rejoining him in Holland in November when she had recovered. She later claimed not to have known that George and his associates were spending their time on the Continent committing fraud. George and Nelly spent one day at the Victoria Hotel in Rotterdam before travelling on to Haarlem, where they met up with Austin and Mac. George and Nelly then booked into a hotel in Haarlem as husband and wife.[8] On most days George took the twenty-eight-minute rail journey from Haarlem to Amsterdam, leaving after breakfast and returning for dinner at five o'clock.[9] Their stay in Haarlem lasted for about two weeks in all.

At the end of their trip to the Continent, Austin and Mac returned to England by way of Calais, while Nelly and George travelled home on 15 November via Harwich. They reached the Alexandra Hotel in London on 16 November, where they once again met up with Mac. They only stayed three nights before moving on again to Ford's Hotel in Manchester Square. They were living life at such a fast pace that it must have had Nelly in some-what of a whirl. When Edwin Noyes first arrived in London to become part of the fraud on the Bank of England, he was intro-duced to Nelly as 'Mr Howe, from Liverpool'.

The Americans were constantly aware of the danger posed by people finding out too much about them and their daily practices, hence the frequent changes in lodgings. Charles Wyatt, a waiter at Ford's Hotel, went to George one day and offered him a copy of *The American Register*. Much to his surprise, George responded by saying that he was not an American. This puzzled the waiter because he had heard his accent previously.[10] The first time Wyatt saw Austin and Mac was when they arrived at the hotel to visit Mr and Mrs Bidwell. As they were out at the time, he was reluc-tant to let two strangers into their room, so he asked the gentlemen to wait in the hall. Then, however, he noticed the resemblance between George and Austin and asked Austin 'if he was the brother to whom he had posted some letters'.[11] Austin admitted that he was and then Wyatt allowed them to wait in the room. When Wyatt was apologetic about not letting them in at first, Austin tried to put him at ease by saying: 'It's all right, you are working on the same principles as we are.'[12] The two men then asked for some sealing wax and a candle and they sealed up a parcel, which they left for George. Wyatt saw Austin and Mac at the hotel a number of times after that and he remembered Mac having dinner there on 21 December. George also had Wyatt send a telegraph for him to a Captain Bradshaw at the Grosvenor Hotel 'a few days before Christmas', obviously utilizing one of their aliases for communication.

For Christmas 1872 no expense was spared. George Bidwell and Nelly hosted a lavish dinner party at Ford's Hotel for Austin, Mac and Noyes, along with two lady friends. George asked Nelly to purchase Christmas presents for the others, leaving the choice of items to her own discretion. She went to Messrs Bowring and Arundel in Bond Street, where George kept an account, and bought four silk neck scarves.[13] She also added the extra touch of having the initials of the recipients embroidered on each of them. For the ladies, who arrived late to the party, she had purchased some fashionable gloves.

Noyes dined with them again at Ford's Hotel on 27 December and paid yet another visit the following morning. In the new year, on 1 January 1873, they were on the move once again; perhaps the curiosity of Charles Wyatt and his co-workers had become a little too uncomfortable. George and Nelly checked out of Ford's Hotel and he asked that his letters be directed to Nelson's Hotel, Great Portland Street. The staff at Ford's were used to him receiving letters addressed to 'George Macdonnell, Esq.' and he asked that these too be redirected to the same address.[14] Two or three letters did arrive after their departure and were sent on as requested.

This time, despite the forwarding address of Nelson's Hotel, George and Nelly actually moved to lodgings at 87 Upper Gloucester Place. It was while living there that Nelly had good cause to become suspicious that her lover was not perhaps as respectable a businessman as he liked to pretend. She came across a rather large sum of money stashed away at their home:

... I saw a leather bag. I kicked it, and found it contained money. I saw it opened, and there were three or four canvas bags full of money in it. George Bidwell had brought it, and I believe he took it away next day. He did not say where it came from. He knew that I had seen it.[15]

This was not the only time that Nelly would see a ready supply of cash at Upper Gloucester Place:

> While at Upper Gloucester Place I saw some bank notes in the possession of Macdonnell – three, for 500*l*. each. He took them from his pocket in the presence of George Bidwell and the servant. I got hold of one of them and put it, by way of a joke, into my pocket, upon which Macdonnell asked me to return it, saying it was all the money he had in the world. I then gave it back to him. He had previously asked me if I had ever seen a 500*l*. note before, and I said I never had.[16]

Nelly opted not to concern herself about such matters. Perhaps she was enjoying spending George's money too much to make a fuss.

Noyes was not long in London until he too had a romantic interest. He had become involved with Miss Ellen Franklin. When he first met Ellen he introduced himself as Edwin Hall from Newark, a businessman who had just come over from America three weeks earlier. He had come to England, he told her, to introduce a new model of milking machine. She might not have known anything about milking machines, but it was soon clear to her that he was doing very well for himself financially: among the items he bought for her was a sealskin jacket costing £11 10*s*.[17] Before long they decided to move in together. On Sunday 2 February Ellen Franklin took Noyes to the house of Mrs Sarah White located at 7 Charlotte Street, Fitzroy Square, to look at potential lodgings on the drawing-room floor. She had already visited the place herself and thought it suitable. Noyes agreed and they soon moved in. Shortly afterwards, Ellen noticed how Noyes had begun referring to himself, using her name, as 'Mr Franklin'.

Noyes' usual routine was to leave the house every morning between eight and ten, and return in the evening for dinner. Ellen Franklin grew somewhat curious about his business dealings and two boxes full of his possessions eventually proved too intriguing for her to resist. On Monday 24 February, she opened one of these boxes and found 'a roll of American bonds, enclosed in an envelope'.[18] She even showed them to her landlady, Sarah White, and her landlady's husband, Jesse White, who arrived home while the women were looking at them. Mr White noticed that many of the bonds were to the value of $500 and 'they were thickly rolled together'.[19] He estimated the value of the roll to be around £3,000 to £4,000. Rather wisely, he advised Ellen to put them back where she had found them. Inside the same box she also found a pocket book with the name Noyes written on it, which she did not recognize, as well as two envelopes: one of these was addressed to the name Horton, and the other to Noyes at room number six, Terminus Hotel, London Bridge.[20] She saw that one of the envelopes had a cheque for £125 inside. By the time Noyes returned with Mac, she had followed Jesse White's advice and put everything back inside the box. Nevertheless, Noyes must have become aware of her snooping because that very evening he took action:

... he packed up the bonds in some very strong paper, and tied it with string, sealing it also with some crystal cement and a seal, upon which were the initials 'E.H.'.[21]

The following morning he took the parcel away with him, telling Ellen that 'he was to send it by mail train to Stafford to some friends of his'.[22] Although she was very curious about what she had found in the box, Miss Franklin, like Nelly Vernon, would later claim that she had been completely unaware that her lover was involved in any criminal activity.

Mac had lived at a number of different locations around London including, for a time, the Grosvenor Hotel. For a few days from the end of January until early February 1873, he stayed at Edwards' Hotel, George Street, Manchester Square. His room had been booked the day before his arrival by George and they met there practically every day. Then, on 6 February 1873, he moved into a private hotel run by Miss Agnes Belinda Green at St James's Place and it is here that many of the forged bills were produced. When Mac first took the rooms there, he told the manager, Franz Antoine Hérold, that 'he had just come from a very hot climate in

South America' and 'would always require a very large fire in both sitting-room and bedroom'.[23] The hotel staff obliged by keeping the fires going at all times. Mac also demanded that the staff knock loudly at his door and wait until given permission to enter. George arrived there most days around eight o'clock in the morning and they would spend hours working on the forgeries, burning any incriminating waste paper in the fire. They used the gas burners so much for necessary light that all the glass globes cracked.

Nelly complained that as George was having breakfast so early, and presumably waking her in the process, he would be better having it at Mac's place instead, which he mostly did from then on. During this time George went off on his frequent trips to Birmingham, sometimes telling Nelly that he was going to Rugby. George and Nelly continued to have Austin, Mac and Noyes around frequently for meals at Upper Gloucester Place.

The reality was that the exceedingly good time being enjoyed by the Americans in London could not last for ever and they knew it. When the first of the forged bills of exchange that they had sent to the Bank of England reached their due date, they would then be removed from the bank vault and sent off for payment. At that point Mr Frederick Albert Warren would be exposed as a cheat and a forger. They knew that they would have to act before this happened, by bringing the lucrative scam to a close and going home to America with their substantial profits. They began to make preparations.

On 25 February 1873, George and Nelly left their lodgings at Upper Gloucester Place and moved to the Albemarle Hotel. When they were leaving, George instructed Nelly to lie to Mrs Groves, the landlady at Upper Gloucester Place, and say that they were leaving London altogether. The distinct impression was to be given that their destination was the Continent rather than The Albemarle. Of course, their ultimate destination was America. Nelly, not understanding the true nature of what was going on, was somewhat puzzled and annoyed by the subterfuge in which she was being asked to partake:

George Bidwell told me to say [at the Abermarle] that Mr Macdonnell had taken the rooms, and that he (Bidwell) and I had just come from Paris. I said I thought there was no need to tell a falsehood about it, and the statement would be ridiculous. He replied that as 'Mac' had said so we had better say the same.[24]

Nelly believed, rather naively, that George was not pleased that Mac had used such an elaborate tale to explain their arrival, but once it was done he had no other option but to go along with it. The fact that she was concerned about such a trivial matter as this indicates that Nelly was blithely unaware of what lay ahead.

CHAPTER 15

The Missing Dates

On the morning of 1 March 1873, George and Noyes met at Garraway's Coffee House, as they often did, in order to discuss the transactions that were to be carried out that day. They had plans to purchase US bonds from Messrs Jay Cooke, McCulloch and Co. and make a deposit in the Horton account. Of course, once Noyes reached the Continental Bank everything changed. Whether it was carelessness, arrogance or just misfortune that led to two forged bills of exchange being sent to London without a date included is hard to know, but that is what led to Noyes' arrest. For Noyes himself, another annoying fact was that they had already performed a test transaction that morning without any difficulty:

> As was our usual custom, we sent a commissionaire with a small check to be cashed, to see if the way was all clear. The check was for £4. I watched him into the bank. The clerk handed over four sovereigns at once, only just glancing at the check.... all seemed propitious.[1]

Of course, once arrested, Noyes did stick to the plan and declared his innocence vehemently. He was, he claimed, nothing more than an employee of Mr Horton and knew nothing of the intricacies of the man's business dealings. At first the staff and manager of the Continental Bank backed him up in this. After all, they believed his story to be true. The police, however, were highly suspicious about this young American from the beginning.

George first found out that matters had gone awry in a rather bizarre fashion: as he walked along the street he actually met Noyes being led to Bow Lane Police Station by his captors. The two fraudsters passed each other on the street without, of course, either man acknowledging the other in any way. Even though George was understandably shocked by the scene and the unmistakeable realization that something had gone wrong, the experienced thief did not panic. He gathered himself; he was sure that Noyes would portray himself as an innocent employee, just as they had planned, and he believed firmly that it would be impossible for the police to link either Mac or himself to the crime. Austin, of course, was already out of the country.

Nevertheless, he was well aware of the potential dangers inherent in the fact that Noyes was an American and they were also Americans. In a crime this big, all Americans in London would be under suspicion. He knew that it was prudent for both he and Mac to leave the country as soon as they could without attracting attention. The first thing they had to do, though, was tidy things up and make sure they destroyed any incriminating evidence left lying around. With this in mind, George met Mac at his lodgings at Miss Green's Hotel in St James's Place, Piccadilly.

Mac then went to Noyes' lodgings where he found Ellen Franklin expecting her man to return home soon. Although Noyes had told her that he would be back around 2 p.m., Mac explained to her that something had come up and he would now be away from home 'for a week or two'. He then removed everything from the lodgings that he thought might be incriminating.

George advised Mac to continue living at his lodgings at Miss Green's Hotel for a while because an American moving address suddenly could attract the attentions of the police. Mac agreed at first but then his nerve must have failed him because on 3 March he moved out. He told the staff at Green's that he was going to Paris but would be back in London the same night. Manager Franz Antoine Hérold told him he thought that was impossible, but Mac replied that 'he was a very quick traveller'.[2] In fact, the manager advised him not to travel at all that day because of the inclement weather, but Mac was insistent. He told him that a friend would pick up the City Directory and the Continental Railway Guide that he had left behind.

Leaving the lodgings in that way was a mistake. When his land-lady, Miss Agnes Green, read in the *Daily Telegraph* about the forgeries committed by the American Mr Warren, she wondered if there was a connection between that event and the sudden depar-ture of her nice American lodger. There was, after all, a handsome reward on offer and she decided to contact the police.

Miss Green was able to inform the police that her American lodger had been visited frequently by other Americans. They searched the room that had been occupied by her lodger and found a number of items that George and Mac had overlooked. There was a piece of blotting paper on which were left some marks that were decipherable to the investigators. Among the information read from this piece of blotting paper were a number of terms relevant to the investigation:

> 'Accepted payable at,' 'London and Westminster Bank,' 'The Bank of Belgium and Holland,' 'Ten thousand,' 'St. Petersburg,' 'A. Biron,' 'Schroeder and Co.,' 'C. E. Dalton,' 'F. A. W.,' and many others less distinct.[3]

These marks were interpreted by the investigators to include, among other items, the impressions of the writing on a cheque made out on the Horton account, later cashed by Noyes, the details on a cheque drawn on the Warren account at the Bank of England and a letter sent to Austin in New York, which contained £2,700.[4] They also found an address in Pimlico that turned out to be that of Daisy, the barmaid from the Turkish Divan. There was a London City Directory from which the pages listing entries on engravers, printers and such like had been removed, as well as those giving 'the names of the governor, directors, and officers of the Bank of England ... [and] the names of certain merchants and bankers'.[5] Some of the tradesmen whose listings had been removed became a fruitful part of the investigation.

The staff at the hotel were able to supply other interesting facts: the reason the globes in the gas lights were all cracked and black marks could be seen on the ceilings above the burners was because the gas lights had been kept burning for so long and at such a high pressure. The manager, Franz Hérold, told them that the gentleman 'was always writing in the bedroom, and with the blinds down'.[6] He had given the lodger a piece of glass to replace a globe that had cracked in the burner. The American always wanted a big fire burning in his room, Mr Hérold said, because he had just come from South America and felt the cold in England. In fact, he complained because the fires were never big enough for him.[7]

CHAPTER 16

On the Move Again

O n 3 March 1873, George and Nelly left the Albemarle
Hotel and travelled to St Leonards, near Hastings, where
they booked into a suite of rooms at the Royal Victoria Hotel.
George had still not told Nelly what was going on, although
the sense of urgency now being displayed by both him and Mac
must have been palpable. Nelly and George were seen off from
Charing Cross Station by Mac. Understandably, George had left
no forwarding address at the Albemarle. Arriving at St Leonards
around midday, George booked some additional accommodation
at the hotel for Mac, telling the staff that his friend was due to
arrive by a later train. He also asked that, as his friend would have
a box of clothes that needed airing, 'a large fire' be lit in the gentleman's room.[1] This, of course, was to facilitate yet more burning of
potential evidence. George then travelled to the station by fly to
collect Mac, who arrived with 'a trunk and other luggage'.[2]

That night George, Nelly and Mac dined together at the Royal
Victoria and then, at nine o'clock, George and Mac went to Mac's
room where they spent hours together busily making plans and
burning evidence. When a hotel employee, Alexander Naylor,
arrived to dust the room at seven o'clock the following morning,
they sent him away.[3] At 10 a.m. they all had breakfast together.
Then they sent for a locksmith to get a lock picked, no doubt to
Noyes' locked trunk. At twelve o'clock Macdonnell checked out
of the hotel and, according to the staff, left with 'much more
luggage than he had brought'.[4] Alexander Naylor heard him ask
the fly driver to take him to Hastings. Then, about an hour later,
Mr and Mrs Bidwell also left, with some more luggage, asking

their driver to take them to the post office in Hastings. The staff noticed, after they had left, that there was 'a quantity of burnt paper in the grate'.[5]

George and Mac now had an urgent need to get as much of their money as they could over to America. With this in mind, on 5 March 1873, Mac took one of their trunks to the London office of the North Atlantic Express Company at Moorgate Street and had it sent to the fictitious 'Major George Matthews' in New York.[6] He gave his name and address as 'Charles Lossing, Tunbridge Wells' and claimed that the trunk contained only 'wearing apparel'.[7] He was charged £3 2s. for its transportation to New York. It did contain some 'wearing apparel', as Mac had stated, but hidden inside were also two watches and, far more importantly, $220,950 worth of United States bonds all tidily wrapped up in 'soiled linen'.[8] Amazingly, there was also a car plate inside displaying the name 'George Bidwell' and one of George's cards.[9] The North Atlantic Express Company, New York, received a letter on 8 March concerning this trunk, giving instructions as to its collection. That letter came from Nelson's Hotel in London and was signed 'G. Matthews'.[10] It had been written by George.

The trunk arrived at the North Atlantic Express Company's offices at 71 Broadway, New York, on 19 April. A woman calling herself Mrs George Matthews arrived subsequently with an order for the trunk's collection signed by George Matthews, but she was not permitted to take it away.[11] The Pinkerton Detective Agency had made sure that not only the post office but also the transport companies were all on the lookout for letters and packages that might be connected with the fraud. Therefore the trunk was opened by the authorities and the contents handed over to 'the Receiver of the Supreme Court under an attachment by the Bank authorities'.[12] It was another breakthrough in the case:

> The police authorities in New York have recently, in connexion with the Bank of England forgeries, made a most valuable recovery of bonds in which the proceeds of those forgeries were invested. A trunk ... addressed to 'Major George Matthews, New York,' came over in the steamer Cuba, and was ordered to be left at the New York office of the company

until called for. On the 19th of April a woman calling herself Mrs George Matthews presented an order for the delivery of the trunk signed 'George Matthews'. In the meantime information had been received that this trunk was really the property of George Bidwell, and orders had been given for its detention, so it was not given up. Yesterday, the 21st, the trunk was taken possession of, under an order of Court, by Mr Jarvis, the Receiver in the case, and upon being opened and examined it was found to contain a quantity of wearing apparel, two watches, a number of other articles, and three packages of United States' Bonds rolled up in soiled linen, and amounting in all to $220,950. These bonds were found to be identical with those advertised in London as having been obtained through the forgeries. From memoranda found in the trunk it was shown that it had been shipped by and belonged to George Bidwell.[13]

On Wednesday 5 March, George and Nelly went to Dover where George paid a visit to the local bank. Under the name Mr James E. Smart he got a bank draft for £300 in exchange for which he gave gold.[14] This £300 was intended to pay for Noyes' defence and was, subsequently, paid into the account of his solicitor, Mr Howell.[15] As they travelled by train from Dover to Canterbury, George handed Nelly a luggage ticket, which he told her to look after. He did not tell her anything about it but it was a ticket that could be used to gain access to a box that had been in the possession of Noyes and was now deposited at Charing Cross Station waiting room.[16] George returned to London alone while Nelly went back to Hastings, where she spent the night. The following morning she paid their hotel bill with £20 that George had given her, and then returned to London with the remaining luggage.

The next morning, back in London, George took breakfast at Nelson's Hotel and on leaving he asked his friend, the manager Kate Mary English, to hold on to his bag and coat for him. In the afternoon a cabman arrived with a note from George and collected the bag and coat.[17] When George met Nelly at Charing Cross Station later that day, she noticed that he had cut his moustache short. He hailed a cab for them and, as he travelled 'a short distance' with her, gave her instructions about taking the luggage to Fenton's Hotel in St James's Street and then his dressing case to her lodgings in Duke's Road, where he said he would meet her. He then got out of the cab and Nelly did as she was asked, taking rooms at Fenton's Hotel under the name 'Mrs Bidwell'.[18] She left the luggage in the rooms.

In the end George did not meet her at Duke's Road. Instead, a note was delivered telling her to meet him at Marble Arch with the dressing case instead. This time when she met him he was completely clean shaven and he told her that he was 'in a bother, that some friend of his had been doing something, and he did not wish his name mentioned'.[19] They got a cab to both the Euston Hotel and the Victoria Hotel and each time he sent her in to inquire if there were any telegrams waiting for him. There was only one, which she herself had sent to him some time earlier. Then they went on to Drummond's Hotel.

Later that same day Nelly had the luggage collected from Fenton's Hotel and brought to her. Following George's wishes, she opened the portmanteau with the key, which was in her possession, and 'took out two canvas bags containing money and put them into a small black bag'.[20] Later she met George in a cab and gave him one of those small black bags of money, along with his dressing case. Sometime later, she and Mr Meunier, or 'the little Frenchman' as she called him, took the rest of the money to George at Drummond's Hotel. George now told her that they were going to America. He instructed her to be 'at the Euston Square Station in time to catch a train for Holyhead'.[21] She was to meet him at Holyhead with the money:

Bidwell told me at Drummond's Hotel, on the evening upon which I was arrested, that he was going to America, and I was to meet him at Holyhead with the money.[22]

Later, Nelly and Meunier did just as he had instructed. They made their way to the station, taking the money with them. According to Nelly, Meunier's instructions had been to accompany her to Holyhead in order to 'take care of the luggage'.[23] What Nelly did not know was that by now they were being watched by Sergeant

Spittle of the city police. When she and Meunier arrived at the station at 8.30 p.m., they were stopped and the bag searched. It was found to contain £2,715 10s. and the police were convinced that it was connected with the Great Fraud on the Bank of England. Nelly and Meunier were arrested.

One could view this whole operation as a rather cynical ploy by George to protect himself. He left Nelly in charge of the money and was using her to get it back to America. She was expendable. If she had managed to get to the steamer and they had escaped to America, great, but how long would their relationship have lasted over there? Especially since he had a wife waiting at home for whom he seemed to have genuine affection, notwithstanding his fling with Nelly. On the other hand, if Nelly did not make it and was arrested, as actually happened, at least he was still free. It would appear that the contents of the bag were more important to him than Nelly.

CHAPTER 17

The Women Give Evidence

---•·•---

On Friday 14 March 1873, a week after his last appearance, Noyes was brought back to a crowded Mansion House to face the Lord Mayor for a third time.[1] There was increased interest in this session because the news had got out that two female companions of the forgers were to give evidence. On this occasion the barrister Mr Poland had been instructed by Mr Freshfield to act as counsel for the Bank of England and he would be heading up the examination on their behalf from now on. Noyes was once again defended by Dr Kenealy, assisted by Mr Howell. The day began with Dr Kenealy complaining about the treatment that his client had been receiving from the newspapers, in particular the *Daily Telegraph*. He said that that newspaper 'seemed to take for granted that the prisoner Edward Noyes was guilty'.[2] He also denounced as 'utterly false' two claims made by the newspaper: firstly, that someone representing the company of Messrs Rothschild had visited his client in gaol and, secondly, that his client had attempted suicide.[3] He objected to such reports, which 'were of a sensational character'.[4] His complaints received little in the way of sympathy from the Lord Mayor:

> The Lord Mayor said he believed as a rule the proceedings of his court were faithfully reported, and he was in no way responsible for what appeared in the newspapers by way of comment.[5]

Mr Poland, acting for the prosecution, then went on to outline the major points of the case and, in doing so, demonstrated that he already had a good understanding of Noyes' true role in the affair:

> It was obvious that some bold and skilful person should be set to work in the City who would naturally become known, and might, probably, fall into the hands of the police; and that Warren should be kept in the background ... the prisoner undertook that duty deliberately, and it was part of the scheme that, in the event of his being apprehended, he was to set up the defence that he was an innocent agent in it.[6]

Miss Ellen Franklin was then called as a witness for the prosecution and she described her relationship with Noyes from 1 February until 1 March 1873.[7] She explained how he had told her his name was Edwin Hall and that she never knew him by the name Noyes. He told her, she said, that he had only come over from America three weeks earlier. She testified how he soon began using the surname Franklin. She told the court about the sealskin jacket that he bought her for £11 10s., the box of his possessions that she opened while he was out and the American bonds that she had found inside. Mr Poland interjected to say that there were bonds to the value of between £3,000 and £4,000 in their lodgings at that time.[8] Miss Franklin went on to tell the Lord Mayor that her lover's friend, Mr Macdonnell, 'called upon them about six times altogether' and it was obvious to her that the two men were 'on very friendly terms'.[9] She was able to identify Mac from a photograph shown to her in court.

Her relationship with Noyes ended abruptly, she explained, when on the morning of 1 March 1873, he left their lodgings without any luggage and she heard nothing about his whereabouts until his friend Mac arrived some hours later. He informed her that her man would not return until either the end of the following week or the beginning of the week after that. Mac said that he had to send his luggage on to him, as he had not had time to collect it himself. She said that when Mac intimated that he wanted to take the two boxes that contained her man's possessions, she objected and, in the end, he only took the one that was locked.[10] That box had been packed by Noyes 'on the previous Tuesday' with her assistance. Understandably, Ellen objected to the fact that he had not even said goodbye to her, but Macdonnell explained that this was because, on the day that he left, 'he had been called away and had to catch a train'.[11] Neither Mac nor Noyes ever came back. With hindsight, although she did not know Noyes' specific plans, she said that she had noticed something different about his mood before he left: 'About the last week of our acquaintance,' she said, 'I had thought his manner very uneasy.'[12]

She said that apart from the fact that Nelly Vernon was pointed out to her once in a shop, she had never really met her:

I remember being in the shop of Baker and Crisp, in Regent Street, on one occasion when Noyes pointed out a lady who he said was 'Mrs Bradley,' saying she was staying with his friend George. I now [i.e. in court] recognize her as the witness Helen Vernon. [13]

When the time came for Nelly to take the stand at the Mansion House, Mr Poland announced that, although she had already appeared herself in connection with being found in possession of over £2,000 at Euston Square Station, it was not now intended to continue with that prosecution.[14] This was, no doubt, in return for her agreement to testify against the principals in the Great Fraud. Dr Kenealy interjected with an objection to her testifying, stating that evidence was now 'being adduced against Bidwell' without it being shown that he had committed any crime at all. The Lord Mayor ruled that since 'Mr Poland was undertaking to prove the connexion between the prisoner and Bidwell' he would allow him to continue.[15]

Nelly's evidence centred mainly around her personal relationship with George and his activities while he was with her. She told the court that she had first become acquainted with the American in the previous August and that she also knew his brother Austin, and their friends Mac and the prisoner Noyes.[16] She was able to identify Austin and Mac from photographs produced in court. She told how she had first met them when they arrived at the private box occupied by herself and George at Covent Garden Theatre.[17]

Nelly said that when she first got to know George she was living at 11 Duke's Road, Euston Square, and they began seeing each other and dining together every day. She told how they met up with Austin and Mac while on a trip to the Continent in November 1872. In response to questions from Mr Poland, she went through the details of their life together: the various hotels and lodgings at which they had stayed; her meetings with the other gang members, including her first meeting with the prisoner who was identified to her at that time as Mr Howe from Liverpool; and the Christmas party that they had all enjoyed together. Apart from what she had already stated, Nelly claimed not to know very much more about Mr Noyes: 'I never knew what he was, where he was staying, or what he was doing,' she told the court.[18] She remembered the incident at the shop in Regent Street when Ellen Franklin had seen her:

> On one occasion I went to Baker and Crisp's shop, in Regent Street, to buy a silk dress. George Bidwell was in Calais that day. He told me afterwards I had been seen in Baker and Crisp's shop that day. I asked who had seen me. He said a friend of his with whom I had seen him occasionally.[19]

She also gave details about her own and George's rather frantic activities following the arrest of Noyes at the beginning of March, including the trip to Dover. She explained how she had travelled back to London alone after that trip and that when she met George at Charing Cross Station his moustache had been cut short.'[20]

As to being caught in possession of the money at Euston Square Station, she reiterated that Meunier's instructions had only been to accompany her to Holyhead in order to 'take care of the luggage'.[21] She claimed once again that she did not know 'how much money was in the bag, nor where it had come from'. Her belief, she said, was that it concerned business. George, she believed at the time, 'had something to do with banking' and he had told her that 'his income was 2,000*l.* a year'.[22] Apart from that, she claimed, she knew nothing about his business dealings. She testified that she did not know where Austin Bidwell was at present and, in fact, never knew where he lived or where he came from. Similarly with Mac, all she knew was that 'he was a private gentleman living in St James's Place'.[23]

When asked if she intended to make any legal claim to the money that had been in her possession at the station that evening, she replied that she did not. Once Nelly had finished giving her evidence, the Lord Mayor discharged her and ordered that all her clothes and jewellery be returned to her. Both she and Ellen Franklin were described in *The Times* the following day as 'women of loose character'.[24] Their appearance at the Mansion House, however, had given the case a whole new level of interest to the public.

Other witnesses followed in quick succession: George Cooper, waiter at the Terminus Hotel, London Bridge; Albert Gearing, proprietor of the Terminus Hotel; Peter Steinmayer, waiter at the Cannon Street Hotel. All of these witnesses gave evidence regarding the activities of Noyes and the others. Colonel Francis was recalled to the witness box and shown a photograph from which he identified Mr Warren, the man who had opened the account at his branch of the Bank of England back in May 1872.[25]

When they had finished with the last witness for the day, Dr Kenealy once again requested that his client not be remanded in custody. He asserted that the reasons being put forward for doing so were 'unjustifiable'.[26] The Lord Mayor still disagreed, saying that 'he was more than ever satisfied, after hearing the evidence adduced that day, of the propriety of remanding the prisoner'.[27] Noyes was duly sent back to Newgate Prison and the next hearing was set for the following Thursday at 10.30 a.m.[28]

Jules Meunier, the man who had been arrested with Nelly at Euston Square Station, was then brought before the Lord Mayor and Mr Poland stated officially that he was happy to withdraw the charge against him: 'the bank authorities,' he announced, 'believed the prisoner was in no way connected with the persons engaged in the conspiracy to defraud the bank.' Although agreeing to discharge him, the Lord Mayor did admonish Mr Meunier for acting 'very indiscreetly in the matter' and he stated that 'he had only himself to blame for the inconvenience to which he had been put'.[29]

The Times edition of the following day hit back at Dr Kenealy's assertion in the Mansion House that the press had been biased against his client:

> We expressed no opinion which could fairly be interpreted either for or against him; and we should equally have been to blame had we done either. The only purpose of our remarks is

to assist our readers in appreciating the exact results of the evidence adduced, and to indicate its bearings. All that could be said of the last hearing was that the prosecution had proved Noyes to have acted as clerk to Horton, who is supposed to be the principal agent in the Forgeries. It remained to be shown whether he was acting innocently in that capacity, or whether he was cognizant of the alleged conspiracy.[30]

The newspaper also declared that 'The Bank [of England] had written off 77,000*l*. as the amount of their losses by the affair; but the amount of forged bills actually offered by Warren was more than 100,000*l*., and they would all have been discounted but for the strange oversight we have previously explained'.[31]

The police had conducted a search at George and Nelly's recently abandoned lodgings at Upper Gloucester Place, where they found four bills of exchange and what was described as 'a photographic lens'[32] inside a chest of drawers. The public awaited the next development in this intriguing case.

CHAPTER 18

A Very Rare Accomplishment

—•—

Noyes was returned to the Mansion House for the fourth time on Thursday 20 March 1873, and Mr Poland called a number of bank officials who gave detailed evidence regarding the many dubious financial transactions that had been engaged in by the Americans.[1] For example, Henry William Hughes, who worked in the gold weighing room of the Bank of England, said that he recognized Mac from the picture shown to him in court. He also remembered something about his interaction with the gentleman:

> He was very particular about his name being spelt rightly, saying he himself wrote it 'George Macdonnell' and that he had great difficulty in getting people to spell it properly.[2]

Mr Macdonnell, he said, had brought in gold a number of times which he wanted exchanged for notes. Mr Hughes remembered one occasion when the gentleman was kept waiting for half or three-quarters of an hour and became very agitated about what was going on: 'He was very fidgety; he rang the bell once or twice, and wanted to know why he was detained.'[3]

The evidence given by these financial experts showed how sophisticated, detailed and well thought out elements of the plan had been. One writer for *The Times*, for instance, was intrigued by the elaborate scheme that had been used by the fraudsters to hide their illegal money. He said their tactics resembled 'crossing a running stream in order to throw hounds off their scent'.[4] Because of their ingenuity, it was important, he felt, that the main culprits responsible for this crime be arrested:

It is to be hoped ... that the hand which forged the bills so successfully will be discovered. Such a forger is a far more dangerous person than mere agents in passing notes and cashing bills. The skill required is a very rare accomplishment, and the mercantile community would be relieved of some anxiety if the person who is capable of such frauds was arrested.[5]

At one point in the proceedings a row erupted over £300 that had been provided for Noyes' defence. Dr Kenealy brought the matter to the court's attention:

... Mr Howell, the prisoner's solicitor, had received from an eminent attorney a banker's draft for 300*l.* for the purpose of the prisoner's defence ... [but] that draft on being presented was returned by the bankers, and the prisoner had now no means wherewith to meet this charge.[6]

Dr Kenealy said that 'he thought it a very scandalous proceeding on the part of the prosecution'.

In response, Mr Poland referred to the fact that Miss Vernon in her evidence had testified that George Bidwell had gone to Dover with her on 5 March and had, while there, conducted some business at a bank. Miss Vernon claimed to know nothing about that business, but Poland said that he was now in a position to give some information regarding it. He asserted that George Bidwell, under the name 'Smart', deposited £300 in gold that day for which he 'obtained in exchange a draft upon the London and County Bank in London'.[7] That draft, he said, was 'subsequently endorsed to the order of the prisoner' while he was in custody. In other words, Mr Poland was claiming that the £300 being put up to defend Noyes was George Bidwell's money and was 'a part of the proceeds of the forgeries'.[8]

Dr Kenealy objected to this version of events, saying that the money in question was a different £300. It was, he said, the money given to Mr Horton when the agreement to act as a clerk was drawn up between him and Noyes: 'The man Horton,' he claimed, 'or some friend of his, hearing that he was in custody, had thought

George Bidwell, the elder of the two Bidwell brothers who were involved in the Great Fraud on the Bank of England. George was, in effect, the leader of the gang.

From a Photo. by Rodgers, Hartford.

George Bidwell

18 months after release.

Austin Bidwell, the younger brother, played the role of Mr. F.A. Warren at the Bank of England and was described by the *New York Times* as 'one of the most remarkable criminals' ever produced in America.

UXBRIDGE HOUSE.

The Western Branch of the Bank of England at Burlington Gardens
where the fraud took place.

It did not take long for news of the fraud to reach the financial
heart of the city. The headquarters of the Bank of England can be
seen on the left of the picture and the Royal Exchange faces out.

THE ILLUSTRATED LONDON NEWS

REGISTERED AT THE GENERAL POST-OFFICE FOR TRANSMISSION ABROAD.

No. 1774.—VOL. LXIII.   SATURDAY, AUGUST 30, 1873.   WITH EXTRA SUPPLEMENT   SIXPENCE. BY POST, 6½d.

TRIAL OF THE BANK FORGERS AT THE OLD BAILEY.

The trial at the Old Bailey was big news. Shown in the dock with prison warders sitting behind them are Austin Bidwell on the left, George Macdonnell leaning forward to talk to his legal counsel, George Bidwell with his arms folded and, on the extreme right, Edwin Noyes Hills.

Sir Sydney Waterlow, Lord Mayor of London, who presided over the hearing at the Mansion House.

20568 B
4,0771

*Order of Licence to a Convict made under the Statutes 16 & 17 Vict.,
c. 99, s. 9, and 27 & 28 Vict., c. 47, s. 4.*

WHITEHALL,

18th day of *July* 188*7*.

HER MAJESTY is graciously pleased to

grant to *George Bidwell*

who was convicted of *Forgery*

at the *Central Criminal Court*

for the

on the *18th* day of *August*, 18*73*, and was
then and there sentenced to be kept in Penal Servitude for the term of

Life

and is now confined in the *Woking* Convict Prison,

Her Royal Licence to be at large from the day of his liberation
under this order, during the remaining portion of his said term of Penal
Servitude, unless the said *George Bidwell*

shall, before the expiration of the said term, be convicted of some
indictable offence within the United Kingdom, in which case, such
Licence will be immediately forfeited by law, or unless it shall please
Her Majesty sooner to revoke or alter such Licence.

This Licence is given subject to the conditions endorsed upon the
same, upon the breach of any of which it will be liable to be revoked
whether such breach is followed by a conviction or not.

And Her Majesty hereby orders that the said *George
Bidwell* be set at liberty within Thirty Days
from the date of this Order.

Given under my hand and Seal,

Signed, *Henry Matthews.*

TRUE COPY.

Licence to be at large.

*For Chairman of the Directors
of Convict Prisons.*

R & S (23,576a) 500 4—87

The 'Ticket of Leave' granted
to George Bidwell in 1887.

right to return the sum for the purposes of his defence.'[9] Kenealy therefore asked that the £300 now be handed over to his client. Poland countered this by saying that Mr Horton 'was a myth' and that this agreement between him and the prisoner 'was a mere sham'.[10] Horton's real name, he said, was Austin Bidwell, George Bidwell's brother.

To help settle the matter, Richard Shrewsbury Ely, clerk at the Dover branch of the London and County Bank, was called to give evidence of George Bidwell's business in Dover that day. He confirmed the principal details as they had been outlined by Mr Poland. Mr Henry Potter, cashier at the London Joint Stock Bank, was then called and he produced the actual draft for £300 and testified that it had been paid into the account of Mr Howell, solicitor, 112 Cheapside. The reason that it had been refused payment, he said, was because 'an alteration in the endorsement required confirmation from the payee. There was an erasure of one letter in the endorsement.'[11] For now, at least, the Lord Mayor would not release the money.

At the end of the day Dr Kenealy once again petitioned for his client's release, complaining about the lack of 'any evidence affecting Mr Noyes'.[12] The Lord Mayor, on the other hand, stated that 'the evidence tendered that day had, in his opinion, strengthened the case against the prisoner'.[13] Noyes was remanded until the following Friday.

CHAPTER 19

Austin's Cuban Adventure

———•◦•———

As far as George and the others knew, by the time Noyes had been arrested at the Continental Bank and the chaos resulting from that had ensued, Austin was safe back home in America. In reality, however, this was not the case. In the end his getaway would prove to be the most exotic and adventure-filled of all the gang members. Austin had left Britain all right and gone to France as agreed. He had not, however, gone from there back to America as the others had expected. He may have written those loving letters to Daisy back in London, but what neither she nor his criminal associates knew was that he was about to get married in the romantic city of Paris. While in London, he had fallen in love with another young woman of a higher social standing than Daisy, a woman he described as 'an English lady'.[1] His marriage had been arranged to Jane Georgina Mary Devereux, the daughter of a British army officer.

George did know about the existence of the young woman in question and his brother's relationship with her, but he had urged caution on the matter. He told Austin that he should not marry this woman while he was still involved in a life of crime: 'Do not think of marrying her before you are settled in business,' was his advice. 'Go home, and with the money you have, get into some legitimate occupation; then you can marry with a good conscience …'.[2] George believed that following the near-death experience in the train crash in France, Austin was willing to wait, just as he had advised:

> … I now found him very willing to go home, cutting off all connection with the contemplated fraud; also to give up the idea of marriage until he had established himself in business.[3]

In fact, Austin had his own opinion on the matter and was not particularly receptive to his older brother's advice. The train crash, in making him aware of his mortality, as such experiences often do, may have prompted him to go ahead and get married even sooner than he had intended. Whatever the truth, as the others were initiating the bank fraud in England, Austin was preparing to marry his English lover at the American Embassy in Paris. He left England feeling confident that the enterprise at the Bank of England would be a success. He had arranged for his lover and her mother to travel to Paris, and he joined his beloved at the Hotel St James.[4] His wife, he said, was 'a pure-souled woman, who thought me an angel of goodness'.[5] Of course, in reality, he was leading a double life about which she knew nothing:

> There I was, the centre of merry pleasure parties in gay Paris. A young dude, driving my four-in-hand, and yet a criminal, waiting in hourly expectation a telegram announcing success in a great plot ...[6]

When the telegram 'announcing success' did arrive, it was short and cryptic:

> All well. Bought and Shipped forty bales.[7]

This message from his brother told Austin that they had enjoyed success with the first batch of forged bills, a proportion of which was on its way to him. On the following day, Austin received $25,000 in United States bonds, which he then sold for French notes. At midnight, only hours before his wedding, he travelled to Calais where he met George and Mac straight off the steamer from Dover and received another consignment of bonds, notes and gold from them. As they returned to England on the next steamer, still in ignorance of Austin's plans to marry, he went back to his beloved in Paris laden down with the valuable haul. Nelly was not pleased with George when he returned home from his day trip to Calais without the expensive travelling bag that she had bought for him at a price of around £25. He told her that he had given it to Austin.

It was only afterwards that George found out that Austin had given a considerable amount of the money as a gift to his bride's mother. On the Friday, Austin and his bride were married at the American Embassy and afterwards the newlyweds travelled to Normandy, where they spent Saturday and Sunday. Austin told everyone in Paris that his bride and he were bound for New York when, in fact, his real plan was to go and live in Mexico for a year or two. Even though he was happy with how events were progressing back in England, he was a seasoned criminal who was taking no chances. He bought tickets from three different travel agencies for onward journeys.

They travelled to Madrid and from there to Cadiz. The plan was to travel on to Mexico on board the steamer *El Rey*, but unfortunately they were late for the ship, having been delayed by bandits who attacked their train. This, according to Austin's telling of the story, was only one of the many adventures they encountered along the way.[8] They resolved to travel instead on a different ship, leaving from the port of St Nazaire for Veracruz, Mexico. It felt to Austin as if he was starting a new life and he was very excited about it:

> ... I longed to be on blue water with our good ship's prow pointed to the Western World. Then I felt I could begin to enjoy life. I had a charming wife – delightful companion – and once up anchor all my haunting fears would die, and life's pleasures would be mine to the full.[9]

He was drawn to Mexico because of its remoteness and distance from law and order:

> To be in Mexico was like being in the centre of darkest Africa. There was no extradition treaty, no railroads and no telegraph; above all, I had plenty of cash.[10]

Perhaps he really had decided to put his life of crime behind him and start afresh. The ship on which the new Mr and Mrs Bidwell were travelling to Mexico, *The Martinique*, stopped over in Cuba on the way, and they liked Havana so much that they decided to stay for a while. Austin never forgot the possibility of the law catching up with him but he managed to achieve a level of peace of mind by ingratiating himself with the local colonel of police. His reasoning was clear:

> ... if any telegrams came about me he would certainly bring them to me at once for an explanation. Even if my presence became known, and telegraphic orders for my arrest should arrive, no speedy action would be taken and ample time given me to escape.[11]

By now his brother and the others had no idea where Austin was and he knew nothing of the disturbing events about to occur back in London. He was keeping an eye on the New York newspapers, but was reassured by the fact that everything seemed quiet there. Life in Cuba was good: the country was beautiful, the weather was glorious and Austin had plenty of money to lavish on his young wife. She, of course, was completely unaware of his real life and his true profession. Then, one morning, everything changed. Austin was relaxing in a hammock on the veranda of their rented house, in his wife's company, when the servant handed him his edition of the *New York Herald*. He 'could not suppress an exclamation' upon reading one of the prominent articles included that day:

AMAZING FRAUD UPON THE BANK OF ENGLAND!

MILLIONS LOST!

GREAT EXCITEMENT IN LONDON!

£5,000 REWARD FOR THE ARREST OF THE AMERICAN PERPETRATOR , F. A. WARREN

An amazing fraud has been perpetrated upon the Bank of England by a young American who gave the name of Frederick Albert Warren ... it is rumoured that many London banks have been victimized to enormous amounts. The greatest excitement prevails in the city, and the forgery, for such it is, is the one topic of conversation on the Exchange and in the street... . a young man named Noyes, who was Warren's clerk, has been arrested, but it is believed that he is a dupe.[12]

Once the shock had subsided, Austin began to rationalize what he had discovered and look for positives in the situation. He went for a quiet walk on the beach and pondered his options. After all, he thought to himself, they may have arrested Noyes but they would not be able to pin anything on him or the others. He felt sure that Noyes would never betray them. George and Mac should be safe from capture and were already, he felt, on their way home to America. He would remain where he was for now and then, perhaps in a fortnight, travel to Mexico, where he would buy an estate.

As Austin continued to scrutinize the newspapers carefully over the following days, he saw how the story was developing and spreading. There were dispatches from London, editorials and even cartoons in the comic papers, which made the Bank of England the target of their humour. Austin was amused by his wife's opinion on the matter: those 'who had the audacity to rob the Bank of England … ought to have a whipping'.[13]

Austin wanted to leave Cuba with his wife but he did not see the need for any undue urgency; he delayed their departure in order to go on a trip with some friends to a coffee plantation. He took the precaution of telling his servant, Nunn, to meet him at Cajio on the return journey. Nunn would bring news of home, the New York papers and a selection of weapons, just in case danger was awaiting him:

> If on meeting Nunn I found from the papers he brought that there was any sign of danger I would not return to Havana, but would secure a boat, provision it, set sail alone for some port in Central America and send my servant back after my wife.[14]

Austin visited two plantations during his time in Cuba and, although somewhat preoccupied with his own worries, he was concerned about the treatment of the slaves he saw:

> Perhaps all men are cruel when they are absolute masters of the lives and fortunes of their fellows and amenable to none for their acts. Certainly the white Cubans, as a rule, are cruel

masters in all their dealings with their slaves... . During my stay I was invited to visit many plantations, but visits to two were enough for me, there being too many signs on the surface of the brutality that lay beneath.[15]

On the journey home he was met by Nunn in Cajio as planned and he was reassured that everything was normal. He noticed that much of the fuss over the fraud was beginning to die down in the New York papers and he decided that it was quite safe for him to return home. One of the first people he called on, back in Havana, was his friend the police colonel, to make sure there were no recent developments about which he should be concerned. All was fine and he returned home to a warm welcome from his wife. He began to make final plans for their departure for Mexico. Although a steamer was scheduled to depart in two days, his wife had already sent out dinner invitations for the following Thursday and so he decided to delay their departure once again until the next possible date, which was Saturday.

There were many occasions when Austin had contemplated telling his wife the truth about his life of crime, but he had always failed to do so. He wondered whether the time was now right:

> On the day of our dinner I was strongly tempted to give some hint to my wife that I was in some way entangled in a web, but as she was so happy I could not do it, but resolved to wait until we were settled in Mexico, and then to tell her a little, but not all the truth.[16]

The dinner party would turn out to be a most memorable occasion for their guests. Just after eight o'clock, as dinner was drawing to a close, events took a dramatic turn. Austin would always remember the moment:

> The long windows were open, while the warm breeze from the nearby gulf was pouring through the room. The clock had just chimed the quarter when there came a sudden rush of feet over the veranda and through the hall.[17]

A man, who Austin immediately recognized to be a fellow American, entered the house followed by a number of other men. Looking around the room, the stranger walked up to Austin and, much to the surprise of those in attendance, addressed him with the words:

> Mr Bidwell, I am sorry to disturb your dinner party or to annoy you in any way, but I am forced to tell you I have a warrant in my pocket for your arrest upon a charge of forgery upon the Bank of England ...[18]

The man then identified himself as William Pinkerton, of the Pinkerton National Detective Agency, and introduced one of the men in his company as Captain John Curtin. Austin did not know it yet but it was Captain Curtin who had managed to work out where he was. Curtin had carried out interviews with a number of people who knew Austin when he was working on Wall Street. He had often mentioned to people in casual conversation that, had he sufficient money, he would love to live in the tropics. Curtin suspected he might be in Florida and asked for permission to visit there in order to search for him. The permission was granted and while Curtin was there he also made contact with a number of other possible locations where one might hide. One of these inquiries consisted of writing to a doctor in Havana asking about any wealthy Americans that were living there. This led him to Austin's heavenly hideout.

Confronted by his unwelcome visitors, Austin announced calmly to his dinner guests that it was all 'some unhappy mistake' and asked Mr Pinkerton to accompany him to the 'large sitting room' at the rear of the dining room so that they could discuss the matter further. Pinkerton agreed and in the sitting room he sat on the seat offered to him by Austin. Matters proceeded in a very civilized fashion:

'Will you have a glass of wine?' Austin asked him.

'Yes, but I never drink anything but Clicquot,' Pinkerton replied.[19]

Austin sent for the requested high-quality beverage and a servant soon returned with a bottle and several glasses.

What happened next is unclear. According to Austin, he offered Mr Pinkerton a bribe; it was his experience with New York police of that era, he says, that convinced him he had a good chance of being successful.

'You know the power and value of money?' Austin asked rather pointedly.

'Yes, and I need plenty of it,' was the reply.

'I have a fortune there,' Austin told him, pointing to a nearby trunk. 'Sit where you are ten minutes, give no alarm, and I will give you $55,000.'

'Why, sir,' he said, 'that is $5,000 a minute!'

'Yes, and good pay, too,' replied Austin.[20]

Good pay it might have been but the offer was refused and Austin then claims that he attempted an escape, during which he pulled a revolver and one of the investigators was hit a glancing shot but not seriously injured.[21] In the end he was led away to one of the three carriages waiting outside to drive him to the city of Havana. Austin's wife wept as he was taken away, perhaps already doubting the notion that this was a case of mistaken identity. At first there was considerable outrage among the local community, especially the American element, at how such an esteemed gentleman as Mr Bidwell could be treated in this way. That same night, the United States consul-general, Alfred Torbet, arrived at the hotel where Austin was being held to assure him that everything possible was being done to sort out this terrible mistake and to ensure that he, as an American citizen, was being treated with respect. The following morning Austin's friend, the colonel of police, arrived. He was indignant that not only had Austin been arrested but also that he had not been informed of the arrest in advance. He suggested to Mr Pinkerton that the prisoner be released and that he would be personally responsible for presenting Mr Bidwell when required. Luckily for the colonel's reputation, considering what was to happen later, Pinkerton knew better than to accede to his suggestion.

It did not take long for news of Austin's arrest on suspicion of involvement in the infamous Great Fraud on the Bank of England to reach the newspapers in the United States. They were, at first, supportive of their fellow citizen:

The special telegraphic advices which we publish to-day in reference to the arrest and imprisonment at Havana of Bidwell, one of the parties accused of the recent forgeries on the Bank of England, are very interesting, touching the jurisdiction of the Island authorities in this matter... . he is a citizen of the United States of America, and ... his arrest in Cuba is not justified by any extradition treaty with England, nor by any authority ... his case certainly calls for the intervention of the Secretary of State... . Distinguished lawyers and judges ... in conversation with the Herald correspondent, denounced the act as being utterly illegal and without precedent.[22]

However, once the consul-general had made some official inquiries, he informed Austin that Pinkerton was in possession of orders direct from the State Department at Washington and that he could do nothing to have them dropped. The most he could do was ensure that Austin was not held 'in the ordinary prison'. Consequently, the following day, Austin was moved to the police barracks where he was kept under quite comfortable close guard in the lieutenant's room. Austin, for his part, was still very optimistic about his chances of evading justice:

So at last justice had laid hold of me, but I thought it a very shaky hold – so much so that I was confident that I could break away from her, so that she could never weigh me in her balance.[23]

His optimism was based not on the knowledge that there was no extradition treaty in place that could be used to send him to face justice but, instead, on the fact that he was already planning his escape. Mr Pinkerton feared this might be the case and wrote to the British and American consuls to protest about the security arrangements in place at the police barracks. The only result of this protest, however, was for the colonel of police to have him and his men kept out of the barracks altogether. Austin was being treated well by the local police; his wife was allowed to spend most of the day with him and all his meals were brought from the hotel. At Austin's request, the colonel of police had his men bring two of Austin's trunks from the house over to the barracks. This gave

Austin access to the $80,000 that was contained therein. As part of his escape plan, he told his wife to go to Key West in Florida as soon as possible and wait there for a month. If, by that time, she had heard nothing from him, she was to contact his sister in New York and go to live with her until he returned.

Austin made some very close 'friends' among the police who were guarding him by using his well-proven charm and giving them plenty of brandy, cigars and money. On 20 March 1873, it was arranged that at ten o'clock a door, which led to a second-storey window that opened onto the street and was usually locked, would be left unlocked. On the night in question, Austin exited through that window onto a small balcony. The street beneath him was thronged with people. He climbed over the railing and hung there until a space opened up in the crowd below. Then he dropped onto the street, his hand poised on the revolver that had been smuggled in to him. Nunn, who was waiting below, placed 'a big straw hat' on his head and the two men disappeared into the crowd. Austin was led quickly to a house and into a room where 'bushy whiskers' and cloaks were put on both him and Nunn.[24] Austin then handed over '$10,000 in French and Spanish notes' before being led out the back of the house and into a waiting cab. He and Nunn were taken to the station and put straight onto the 10.30 train out of Havana. Before long the news became public:

> Bidwell, the alleged Bank of England forger, escaped from prison, yesterday, by jumping over the balcony. He was partly dressed. He is supposed to be hiding in the city. Bidwell's Havana friends, seeing the impossibility of counteracting, by legal means, the efforts of the British Consul to secure his extradition, undoubtedly planned this affair.[25]

> Advices from Havana state that Bidwell has escaped from prison, and is supposed to be hiding in the city.[26]

Austin's relief at being free was considerable:

> I had for a few brief days been a captive, shut out from nature's sights and sounds, and that brief deprivation awoke in me a

feeling of appreciation for the feast that is everywhere around us spread with a lavish hand. My mind was in a tumult of delight, and I almost forgot I was a fugitive ...[27]

Soon he was out of the city and a few days later he and Nunn arrived by train into the small town of Guisa, where they picked up prearranged fake police passports and gun permits under the names of Parish and Ellis. They were also provided with horses with which to complete the escape: they were about to travel through dangerous country, where any chance encounter with bandits, soldiers or rebels could lead to their capture, robbery or even death. At this stage Austin persuaded Nunn, although not without an argument, to return home to Havana. He had the audacity, through Nunn, to send a message to Captain Curtin:

I told him to see Curtin, to give him my regards and laugh at him in a nice way.[28]

Austin's ultimate plan was to make his way to central America and from there to the United States. He set off walking into the wilderness, wearing his reliable pair of English walking boots on his feet.[29] For protection he carried two revolvers on a belt around his waist and a wooden cudgel fashioned for him by Nunn. Two bottles of water were suspended from a string on his shoulder, while his chronometer hung from another string elsewhere on his body. His pockets bulged with 100 cigars, 300 cartridges, a loaf of bread and 4lbs of dried beef. In valuables he carried three diamond studs and bonds to the value of $10,000.[30] He travelled by day and slept by night. As he went deeper into the wilderness, the idea of joining the rebels that were based in that area amused him:

... I would make myself known to the rebel chiefs as an American volunteer in the cause of Cuban liberty. And, I thought, what a change of scene for Mr F. A. Warren. From the Bank of England to a volunteer in a rebel camp in Cuba.[31]

Following a number of adventures, which he described later in his own writings, he arrived at a small hamlet called San Miguel.

He was running low on food and resolved to buy some provisions. He knew that exposing himself in this way would be dangerous but he had little choice. He entered what was the equivalent of a village shop and, to his horror, found twenty government soldiers staring at him. He tried to greet them calmly, like a person with nothing to fear. He bought some food, said his goodbyes and left. Fearing that the matter would not end there, once he had exited the shop he ran as fast as he could and hid in some nearby bushes. His fear had not been misplaced. Once he had left the shop, the soldiers had obviously decided amongst themselves that this foreign stranger had something to hide:

> ... the soldiers poured out of the shop, an angry and excited mob, buckling on their belts, cartridge boxes and bayonets as they ran. Some had their muskets, others hastened to get them and all save two stragglers rushed out of the town in the direction from which I had entered.[32]

Austin tried to make his way out of the hamlet but when he came to a river, being too hungry to destroy the food that he had just purchased, he opted to return to his hiding place rather than swim across. As he did so, he encountered some women from the hamlet and, in his panic, drew even more attention to himself by saying 'Buenos dias' or 'good morning' instead of 'Buenos noches'. The women told the soldiers which direction he had gone and before long he was in custody.

Twelve days later Austin Bidwell arrived back in Havana as a prisoner on board the gunboat *Santa Rita*. He complained that most of his valuable possessions had been stolen by the soldiers who had arrested him:

> ... my captors began to go through my pockets, and speedily there was a heap of gold and paper money on the barrel ... I had my $10,000 in bonds pinned in the sleeve of my undershirt. This they missed, but found all else I carried. In the meantime there was an eager audience looking on, absorbed in the interest of the scene.[33]

This time, on his arrival back in Havana, he was not afforded the special treatment of being taken to the police barracks, but was incarcerated in the common prison instead. The authorities also made sure that there was adequate security at all times to hold him, including one of Pinkerton's men posted to watch him twenty-four hours a day. His first visitor was William Pinkerton, who brought him a letter from his wife, a box of cigars and a bottle of wine.

Austin may have been back in captivity but, from his point of view, all hope was not yet lost; a great deal of effort was being put into arguing for his release on the grounds of American citizenship. The newspapers were closely watching events in New York, Havana and London:

New York, April 4

Great efforts are being made by the lawyers to obtain the release of Bidwell, and an action for illegal arrest is threatened.[34]

Havana, April 4

The American Consul here demands from the Cuban authorities the release of the prisoner Bidwell, alias Warren, on the ground that he is an American citizen.[35]

Havana, April 10

The British Consul continues to counteract the efforts that are being made to prevent the extradition of Bidwell.[36]

In the end, however, the American government decided to wash its hands of him, perhaps under political pressure from Britain prompted by the Bank of England:

In the case of ... Austin Biron Bidwell, he and his friends for some time past have been making strenuous exertions to get the United States Government to interfere in his behalf on the ground that he is an American citizen, and Consul-General Torbet has applied to Washington for instructions. The Secretary of State has instructed the Consul-General to take no action in the matter.[37]

Eventually, therefore, the legal attempts to block Austin's extradition to England failed and news reached London that he was to be returned to face charges relating to the Great Fraud on the Bank of England:

London, April 12, 1873

To the great gratification of the authorities here, official confirmation is given to the rumour that the Spanish Government has concluded to grant the extradition of Bidwell, now under arrest in Havana. There seems to be no doubt that Bidwell is the mysterious Frederick Albert Warren, and there is a very general curiosity to see him. Many conflicting stories have been published of his extraordinary escape and equally extraordinary capture. *The Times*' report had it that he was mortally wounded, and that he had on his person when captured diamonds to an enormous value, which had disappeared soon after.[38]

Two police sergeants, Hayden and Green, who had been dispatched from London to bring the fugitive back, took him into their custody. Certain personal possessions of Austin were also handed over to them:

... six American bonds of 1,000 dollars each, two for 500, one for 100, 18*l.* in gold, two 5-franc gold pieces, three diamond studs, a pair of gold and amethyst sleeve links, a gold watch, a gold chain, and a seal ...[39]

Sergeant Hayden showed the items to him and Austin confirmed that 'they were quite correct'.[40] In early May 1873, Austin was on his way back to England and an uncertain future.

CHAPTER 20

Mac's Escape

In Austin's absence, the relationship between Mac and Daisy from the Turkish Divan had developed into a romantic one. Although Daisy became intimate with Mac she, like Nelly Vernon and Ellen Franklin, claimed not to have known anything about the fraudulent activities engaged in by her lover. Her knowledge of his day-to-day activities, she said, was only of a most basic kind:

> On one occasion I came into the City with him [Mac] in a brougham. He left me in the brougham, and on his return he said he had been to his bankers. I don't know where that was. When he returned he had some coloured papers – green, I think – in an envelope.[1]

Mac and Daisy were close enough, however that, when the time came for him to flee the country, he wanted to take her with him. He told her that he had decided to leave because of the recent forgery at the Bank of England. He did not declare his involvement in the crime; he just told her that it was because one night while out at dinner he heard someone say in German that 'It was just what an American would do'.[2] He told her that, because of the fraud, many people in London would be prejudiced against Americans now or, as he put it, 'down upon all Americans'.[3] He said it was time for him to leave England and he would like them to go to New York together. Daisy was very taken with the idea and embraced it enthusiastically.

Mac sent letters with money enclosed to New York in anticipation of their arrival there.[4] These letters, like most of the other correspondence that he and the others had sent, were seized by the postal authorities. On 5 March 1873, having stayed at Daisy's lodgings overnight, Mac left early in the morning to prepare for their departure. While he was out, George called to see him. He asked for Mac and expressed concern that he had not met him earlier at the Grosvenor Hotel as arranged. During the day Daisy's ticket for the steamer to New York was delivered. Later she met Mac near the Lowther Arcade; he gave her a £10 note and told her to take a train from Euston Station to Liverpool, from where they would catch the steamer together for New York. He told her that he might meet her at the station, but if not she was to travel on to Liverpool without him. Mac did not arrive at Euston Station and, unfortunately for Daisy, he didn't go to Liverpool either. Daisy was left waiting for him at the North Western Station Hotel in Liverpool with all her luggage and in the end had to return to London.[5]

He had not deserted her on purpose. In fact, he did set off for Liverpool but then, in the belief that he was being chased by the authorities, decided to turn back and head for Chester. He eventually made his way to Southampton where he boarded a boat for France. From there he caught the steamship *Thruingia* bound for New York.[6]

Mac may have been right about being followed because, by now, the authorities, including the Pinkertons, were on his trail. There was a general sense of alert in place in New York:

In New York the police have been on the alert to capture anyone who may be implicated in the crime who has sought to escape by means of the Trans-Atlantic steamers.[7]

Mac was heading straight into trouble because they had managed to trace him to Paris and then on to Brest, where they found out that he had purchased his ticket on the steamer to New York. It was soon established that he was on board the *Thruingia*. As the steamer had not yet docked, a cable was sent ahead to New York for the attention of Superintendent Kelso of the New York police force. It described Mac's appearance and asked that the American authorities detain him on arrival. The Americans were informed that Sergeant Henry Webb would be dispatched immediately to New York with all the legal documents necessary for the prisoner's extradition back to London. In New York a warrant was issued for Mac's arrest and Captain Irving was put in charge of seeing that it was put into effect. The American authorities were told by London that Mac was armed and would be in possession of a stash of jewellery.[8] The Bank of England had their attorneys in New York, Messrs Blatchford, Seward, Griswold and Da Costa, arrange for a writ of attachment to be issued by the New York Supreme Court, which gave them the legal right to claim any items found in Mac's possession. The bank's action created the awkward legal situation according to which the police were responsible for the prisoner while the sheriff's office were responsible for any possessions found on him. This, naturally, created a situation of competition between the two parties.

As the *Thruingia* steamed into New York on 25 March 1873, with its prized passenger on board, Captain Irving and another detective, along with two deputy sheriffs, were situated on a small boat anticipating its arrival.[9] The detectives stole a march on the sheriffs and managed to board the steamer first. They found Mac, arrested him, and searched his belongings:

> On his person and in his trunks were found about $10,000 in gold, two gold watches, and six diamonds, worth probably $10,000 more.[10]

To their disappointment, however, no bonds of any description were found on him.[11] When the sheriffs arrived, they took possession of the valuables. A number of other people on board the steamer were also searched but no further arrests were made. Mac, for his part, declared himself innocent and said: 'You cannot send me back to England on any such charge.'[12] He had a point; the potential legal difficulties associated with his extradition back to England were apparent:

> The Prosecution will now have to produce *prima facia* evidence of Macdonnell's implication in these forgeries.[13]

As soon as the news of his capture reached Louisville, Kentucky, the authorities in that area let it be known that Mac was still wanted there for absconding on a charge of forgery. From his past history, they were not at all confident that his conviction would be achieved in England:

> The men who know him in Louisville are confident in their predictions that he will not be convicted if taken back to England, as he has escaped difficulties and dangers quite as formidable as those that now hem him in.[14]

Their message was clear: give him to us. In the event that the English authorities proved unable to made the charges stick, they wanted him brought back to Louisville to stand trial there.

The policeman from London, Henry Webb, and his colleague, Edward Hancock, arrived in New York in anticipation of being able to take Mac back to London but the question of his extradition would have to be fought out in the New York legal system first. Right at the start, Mac's legal team disputed the very legality of his arrest:

> ... no evidence had been given to show that the crime charged against the prisoner had been committed by him ... [the] warrant was informal and insufficient, and did not properly set out any offense for which he could be arrested, the complaint upon which the warrant was issued being also defective ... the evidence was insufficient to warrant the commissioner in holding the prisoner.... . Macdonnell's counsel will also claim that conspiracy, with which the prisoner is charged, is not one of the offenses embraced in the extradition treaty with Great Britain.'[15]

Daisy did finally get to go to New York, but only because the police took her there to officially identify their suspect. They had found her address, 80 Tachbrook Street, Pimlico, written down at Mac's lodgings in Miss Green's Hotel, and it seems that in order to get her to talk they gave her the distinct impression that he had gone off with another woman. When she appeared at the hearing, according to the American newspapers, she impressed those who saw her and was described as 'fashionably dressed'.[16] She told the American court about her acquaintance with Mac since the preceding December and how she had expected to travel to New York with him. She testified that she had seen Mac 'in company' with the man called Noyes, who was currently being held by the police in London. She also identified a person shown to her in a photograph as 'Theodore Bingham'. Mr Da Costa informed those present that, although she had believed this to be the man's name, his real identity was Frederick A. Warren.[17]

The complex legal argument went on for weeks including, at one point, the spectacle of Mac being discharged on one warrant and then immediately rearrested on another.[18] Aspects of the case were heard before a number of different legal forums including Judge Woodruff at the United States Circuit Court, the office of the United States Commissioner, Joseph Gutman Jr, and the United States District Court under Judge Blatchford. The prolonged legal process seemed to be proving stressful for Mac as he was described as looking 'careworn and dejected'.[19] The press and the public were also growing impatient with the lengthy and intricate proceedings:

> There is a vast amount of delay in the extradition of George Macdonnell, the Bank of England forger, who is under arrest in New York – so much, indeed, that it is the subject of general remark. There is no doubt as to his guilt or identity, yet legal hairsplitting goes on, and day after day the hearing is post-poned, the only apparent object of his counsel seeming to be delay. That he will be sent to England ultimately there is no doubt, but no one can tell when.[20]

Eventually, the American legal system declared that Mac's extradition back to Britain to face charges relating to the Great Fraud on the Bank of England was legal and could proceed. It was clear, from the amount of money and effort that had been expended by the authorities at the Bank of England, how determined they were to have him sent back to London. The case had attracted considerable attention in the city and on 3 June 1873, the final day of the hearing before the United States District Court, *The New York*

Times noted that 'the court had become filled with persons anxious to see the prisoner'.[21] Mac could now be sent back to face the Lord Mayor in London without further delay. He was handed over to Detective Sergeants Webb and Hancock on 4 June.[22]

> The prisoner was sent back to London in charge of the English detectives, to be dealt with according as the courts there decide... . the following receipt was given for him:
> United States of America – Southern District of New York: We the within mentioned and undersigned Henry Webb and Edward Hancock, detective sergeants of the City of London police, do hereby acknowledge the receipt into our hands of the within-named George Macdonell from Oliver Flake, Marshall of the United States for the Southern District of New York. [Dated 4 June 1873][23]

However, even as they steamed away from the United States, it emerged that there was still one final legal formality to be gone through. Rather bizzarely, Mac's last chance of preventing his extradition was ended by Judge Davis in the court of Oyer and Terminer after he had already left the country:

> At the time the argument was proceeding, the steam ship with Macdonnell on board was already plowing the Atlantic eastward.[24]

The legal saga on that side of the Atlantic was finally over.

CHAPTER 21

George's Celtic Escape

A lthough George kept reassuring himself that there was no
way the authorities could connect him to the fraud, he did
formulate a plan of escape for himself and Nelly according to
which they would travel first to Ireland and from there catch the
steamer, the *Atlantic*, sailing out of Queenstown for New York.
Of course that changed when Nelly and Meunier were arrested at
Euston Square Station and he was forced to flee on his own. He
still kept faith, however, with his original plan.

Having arrested Nelly at Euston Square Station, the police, frustrated that they had been unable to find any photographs of
George, hoped that she might be able to supply them with one. She
was, however, unable to comply. Although she had 'often urged
him to have it taken', she told them, 'he never consented'.[1] George
did not realize it at the time but he could have been arrested before
he ever got out of London. Detective Sergeant Smith was at
Charing Cross Station at 8 a.m. on the morning of 6 March 1873,
and he saw a man 'standing near a telegraph pole' wearing a silk
hat but no overcoat.[2] That man was George, expecting Nelly back
from their trip to St Leonards. With the Great Fraud on the Bank
of England on his mind, Smith's attention was attracted by the
man, who seemed to fit one of the descriptions that had been circulated. Yet the policeman was unsure and did not arrest him. At
1 p.m. on the same day Smith saw the same man again and this
time he looked like he could be trying to disguise himself by
wearing 'a black overcoat trimmed with Astrakhan and a low cap'.
He had also trimmed his moustache.[3] Smith was so suspicious of
the man that he had some employees of the Bank of England come

over and take a look at him. When they failed to identify him as one of the forgers, Smith decided to let him go and watched him leave in a cab. Later Smith would realize that his indecision had allowed George Bidwell, one of the most wanted men in the country at that moment, to slip through his fingers.

When it was clear that Nelly was not going to show up as arranged, George, suspecting the worst, decided to take the 9 p.m. mail train from London to Holyhead. He stood back in the shadows, not boarding the train until the last possible moment, fearing that a number of men whom he saw looking out of the waiting-room window were detectives looking for suspicious Americans:[4]

> As the mail was being transferred from the wagons to the train, I took the opportunity to walk through the big gate unobserved amid the rush and confusion. The car doors were all locked, but on showing my ticket to a guard (conductor) he let me into a compartment ...[5]

It was worse than George had thought; contrary to what he had expected, he had already been identified as a prime suspect in the crime and a widespread search was on for him along with a substantial reward having been placed on his head. He sailed at midnight from Holyhead to Dublin, arriving there around 7 a.m. Events were unfolding rapidly; the authorities were searching for 'an American, about forty years of age, of dark complexion, and ... supposed to be in Ireland'.[6] Unknown to George, the Dublin newspapers, on the very morning of his arrival, were full of the affair.

Still unaware of his notoriety, George caught a train to Cork, arriving there around 4 p.m. Walking down the street, a man came up beside him and asked if he had ever been to Cork before. George simply replied, 'Yes,' and walked on. The man, accompanied by another, followed him. George went into a shop and bought some liquorice. As he did so, he saw the same men walk past, 'gazing intently' in at him as they did so.[7] He left the shop and walked on, this time not seeing the men. Their presence had worried him.

Eventually, George reached the ticket office for the voyage to

New York. From there the passengers were transported out to the steam-ships. As he arrived, one such group of passengers was preparing to leave and the place was crowded. Glancing around the office, he noticed the same two men who had been following him earlier, their heads clearly visible behind 'the crowd waiting to see their friends off for America'.[8] George had little doubt now that they were either detectives or investigators of some sort but realized that they were still not quite sure if he was the man they were after. He decided to walk away.

George always enjoyed telling people that the men may have saved his life that day by preventing him from booking his passage to New York. On 1 April 1873, the *Atlantic* struck land at Marrs Head, Prospect Harbour, losing over half of the thousand or so people on board.[9] George would read about it later:

> The most unimaginative of readers can realize the scene and its accessories; the night of pitchy darkness; the driving rain, and the furious gale through which the long, low and laboring vessel was making her painful way into port. Whether screw or rudder failed her, or whether, as we find it hard to believe, her supply of coals had run so low after an eleven days' voyage that her engines had not power enough to keep the ship to her course, in spite of the gale that was driving her on a lee shore, are theories of the disaster which must depend on a later and fuller news. Certain it is, that the catastrophe came with appalling suddenness, and that, if there be any consolation in the reflection, probably one-half of the victims were drowned in their beds.[10]

George hailed a cab and made his way back to the train. In the end, he managed to get out of Cork without being detained by the two unidentified men and, as George told it later, the next few weeks were spent in a chase through Ireland assuming a variety of disguises and just about managing to stay one step ahead of those in pursuit.

It was while spending the night in Lismore Hotel that the scale of George's predicament became known to him for the first time. After his evening meal he went into the sitting room to relax. He began chatting with a gentleman who he assumed, from his demeanour and manner, to be a lawyer. The man was reading the newspaper and, on a number of occasions, offered it to George. Afterwards, when the man had gone to bed, it occurred to George that he had actually worked out his true identity and was trying to tip him off. When George glanced at the newspaper now left lying on the table, there before him in print was proof that his identity was known to the police. What is more, he discovered that they knew he was in Ireland and there was a reward out for his capture.[11] He could hardly believe it:

> I sat for an hour ... utterly dumbfounded, bewildered, para-lyzed. I had experienced some shocks, some 'take-downs,' in my time, but never one to compare with this.[12]

Once he recovered his senses, George put the newspaper straight into the fire. Although it seemed as if his 'lawyer' friend had no interest in helping the authorities, George thought it wise to leave early the following morning just in case the man changed his mind, enticed by the reward.

It was still dark when George left the Lismore Hotel early on Sunday 9 March 1873.[13] He was already on the street when he noticed a man watching him from the other side. The man followed him as he began to walk and it was only by circling the hotel and moving quickly that George managed to evade him. He then roused a rather sleepy owner of the livery stable and by the induce-ment of money arranged for transportation by horse and jaunting car to the town of Clonmel. From there he travelled on to Cahir where, in order to enlist the help of some locals, he pretended to be a Fenian over from America with important papers to be distributed in the cause of Irish freedom.

Later, he made his way back to Clonmel, but while waiting in the railway station for the arrival of the train to Dublin had a risky conversation with a man whom he judged to be 'a local policeman in private clothes'.[14] Although, according to George, the man asked him if he was an American and even stated openly that he was interested in getting the £500 that was on offer for the capture of the parties responsible for the great forgery in London, George managed to convince him that he was not an American. After that George resolved to turn himself into a Russian, who could only speak the bare minimum of English.

He managed to arrive safely in Dublin late into the night.[15] George's vigilance and fear regarding being identified and captured in Ireland were not without validity. He saw stories in the newspapers regarding the efforts being made by the authorities in Ireland to catch the suspect or suspects and there were even reports of arrests having been made:

> Three shabbily dressed men who, from their accent, are believed to be Americans, were arrested in Cork, Ireland, this morning while attempting to deposit $12,000 in that city. They are supposed to be the parties who recently committed the frauds on the Bank of England.[16]

These cases of mistaken identity were happening not only in Ireland but also in other countries, as testified by a letter written to the editor of *The Times* from a very disgruntled ex-sheriff of London and Middlesex, Charles W.C. Hutton, who had been mistaken for Mr C.J. Horton on the run in Germany:

> Myself and son, a sub-lieutenant, R. N., made a great attempt to reach the grotesque old city of Nuremberg on Saturday last, 8th March, arriving there about 7 p.m. We were asked to put our names in the stranger's book, as usual, which we did, and retired to bed. Imagine our surprise, on rising on Sunday morning, at receiving a visit from one of the chief police officers requesting us to 'legitimize ourselves'. I asked him his object for making this demand, when he replied that a man named 'Horton' was wanted by the English police. In vain I showed him an old passport and letters addressed to me showing that my name was Hutton; he informed me that I could not leave my room, and placed two policemen at the door. At 1 o'clock I remembered an influential inhabitant of the town who knew me, and I sent for him. He at once went to head-quarters and gave bond for me to a large amount, and at 6 o'clock in the evening myself and son were released. You

will remember that in the case of Dr. Hessel four persons swore to his identity before he was deprived of his liberty. In my case a similar name to that required was sufficient to deprive me of mine.

I have since received, thanks to the strenuous and prompt action of the British Minister at Munich, a very ample apology in writing for the blunder that had been committed; it is signed by the Burgermeister of the city, and, as the intelligence of this worthy seems to be equalled only by his simplicity, he sends me a safe pass to protect me in my further travels, in case Hutton should again be considered the same as Horton.[17]

A few days later and having, according to himself, narrowly avoided a number of other near captures, George was on the train heading for Belfast via Drogheda. By this time he was using the disguise of a Frenchman. Once again he found himself involved in a discussion about the Great Fraud that had taken place in London and the fugitive that was reportedly on the loose somewhere in Ireland. 'I tell you those Yankees did a clever thing when they attacked that powerful institution,' he reported one man in the train carriage as saying to him. 'The one they have got penned up here in Ireland can't possibly escape; indeed, according to the newspapers, he is already in the hands of the police. I am almost sorry to hear it, for in getting the best of that bank so cleverly the rascal deserves to get off.'[18]

No matter what the newspapers were reporting, George was still not in the hands of the police and he eventually managed to escape from Ireland to Scotland, catching a steamer from Belfast. First he went to Glasgow, and then, on 10 March 1873, arrived in Edinburgh. The following day he knocked at the door of 22 Cumberland Street, the house of William and Ann Laverock, where he enquired of Mrs Laverock whether she had a room to let. All he required, he told her, was a simple room with a bed. She said that she could put a bed into a sitting room and he could have that if he wanted. As it happened, the room was ideal for George as it looked out onto the street. He took the room under the name 'Mr Coutant', saying that he had just travelled from the continent of Europe to Scotland on business. He asked her if she had any

French or German lodgers staying with her at that time and she replied that she had not. While in Edinburgh he decided to pretend to be 'of French extraction' and although he always spoke to his landlady in English, it was with a foreign accent. Ironically, Mrs Laverock never thought it was a French accent.[19]

On 11 March George sent a letter from Edinburgh to Mac in New York, telling him how things were going. He addressed it to Alfred John Watson, Post Office, New York, a false identity that they had agreed upon in advance. His false assumption was that Mac, by then, was safe in New York:

11 March, Edinburgh.

Dear M.,—Your Irish friends were too warm for me, but I avoided their attentions by coming over here, and shall remain quietly here until I hear from you. I had less money than I supposed, and have only, say 7*l.* on hand, but have 400*l.* in valuables, but do not care to offer anything at present. You better send me 100*l.* in English or French bank notes, not by registered letter, dividing it into three sums, one letter here, one to Copenhagen, one to Barcelona, all directed same name as on this. Do not telegraph. It may be some time before I reach home. Will write often, directed same name as this, but to Brevoort.[20]

On 13 March 1873 he wrote to Mac again and seemed remarkably calm, saying that he intended to make a dash for home (i.e. America) in a week or two:

I think you need have no more anxiety on my account, as I feel quite sure of keeping my health intact. I send you a batch of news herewith, which I know will surprise, if not please you, and as I am in rec[eip]t. of the papers, will keep you posted. I am very quietly and comfortably situated here, and shall remain for some days in status quo ... in case I conclude to dispose of some valuables I have about me, I shall make a dive for home in one or two weeks longer; of course I have no news of poor Nell, but think she will do well for herself, and can't imagine on what grounds they hold on. Of course it was foolish for me to leave L[ondon] ... Your friend has had a series of the most extraordinary adventures since you saw him, a hell's chase, and no mistake. His nerve has stood him through two taps on shoulder, and four encounters. He has been a Fenian, a Priest, a Professor, a Russian, who could speak only '*veree leetle engles, mais un peu de Francais et Allemand*', a deaf and dumb man with a slate and pencil – all in the space of a week.'[21]

He enclosed newspaper clippings with this letter concerning reports of Noyes' appearances at the Mansion House. He wrote to Mac again on 15 March telling him about the numbers of their bonds being printed in the newspapers and making plans to get Nelly away from London to New York in order to prevent her from giving evidence:

I forgot to mention that the Nos. of those 50 are advertised, which you bought, so you can act accordingly... . I think I shall remain quiet until I hear from or see someone. It may be best to send someone over to get Nelly out of the way. Let someone go and tell her I have sent for her to come over to N. Y. She will come at once... They can get track of her at 11, Duke's Road, Euston Road, St. Pancras Church. You may also write to Mr. Anthony, 21, Enfield Road; also same name here, directed Post Office, Pitt Street. You may mail me money, but send no one to me, as I will trust no one except my brothers. Don't on any account use the telegraph.[22]

There was a marked deterioration in George's mood when he wrote to Mac again on 18 March. This time he enclosed a printed notice from *The Times*:

Further caution. Bankers, Brokers, and others, are hereby cautioned against accepting, receiving, negotiating, or otherwise dealing with all or any of the undermentioned securities of the U.S., the same having been obtained by means of forgery.

The notice listed the relevant numbers and asked anyone with information to contact an Inspector Bailey at the police station, Old Jewry. In the letter dated 18 March George also enclosed the notice offering a £500 reward for the arrest of either himself, Austin or Mac, and a report on the appearances of both Nelly and Ellen Franklin at the Mansion House.[23] His intention was still to go to London soon in order to get Nelly:

> It made me nearly sick to read what I enclose ... I shall try to get hold of Nelly, although I may incur some risk by doing so; yet I shall be most cautious in my movements. I am fairly stuck for want of money, and cannot put up anything at present, so I shall lie quiet here for a few days and then go to London ... I have yet over 5*l*. It is all right as long as I keep inland, but the moment I touch the borders there is the devil to pay. I ran through an awful gauntlet last week. Of course I should not have got Nell and myself into this dam stew... and who would have dreamed they would take hold of her that way... . Of course it is impossible to say what move, or when I shall make one, but my present opinion is that I shall be in London when this reaches you.

George suspected, by now, that the authorities must be intercepting their mail:

> The telegraph, and I suspect the post also, is an open book for these parties. I suppose they have procured special permit... . You must keep a list of letters you send, as they may not reach me. You must have 50,000 dollars ready to use for bail, if needed.[24]

George was very serious about this audacious plan to return to London. He wrote to his former landlady, Mrs Ann Thomas of 21 Enfield Road, as Mr Anthony, and told her that he would like to return to her house for a while and inquired whether she had any rooms available. She replied to him at Pitt Street Post Office, Edinburgh, using the stamped addressed envelope that he had sent her, informing him that, regrettably, she was full at that time, but could arrange a place for him to stay with a neighbour.[25] But the truth is that before he could make any trip to London, things were about to get very dangerous for him in Scotland.

George was correct to use aliases, false addresses and cryptic messages in his correspondence whenever he could, because those in authority at the United States' postal service were co-operating fully with the investigation and had, as he suspected, already intercepted a number of the gang's letters. Once such letter had been addressed to 'A. Biron Bidwell, Esq., New York, U.S.A., care of New York Safety Deposit Company, 140, Broadway, New York'. It was posted originally at Cannon Street, London, on 25 March 1873, and bore the postmark of New York dated 13 March. It was sealed with wax.[26] Inside the envelope was over $20,000 in US bonds.[27] Another letter addressed to 'G. C. Brownell, Esq., Brevwort House, Fifth Avenue, New York' was also intercepted. It bore 'the Cork postmark of the 7th March, and that of New York of the 20th March'.[28] Brevwort House was an upmarket hotel in New York. This letter bore the same seal as the other one and contained bonds to the value of $17,500.[29] A third letter had the postmarks 'Edinburgh, March 11' and New York, March 24' on it with the address 'George M. Macdonnell, Esq., Post Office, New York City, U.S.A'. Once again the same seal was used.[30] This time the letter was unsigned but it quite clearly gave Mac instructions on how to 'apply for the letter addressed to G. C. Brownell, at the New York post-office'.[31] All of this intelligence that the investigators were gathering was making the evasion of capture that much more difficult.

CHAPTER 22

The Suspicious Frenchman

---◆---

It became George's habit to buy daily newspapers from Mr Gardner, a newsagent in Dundas Street, Edinburgh, so that he could remain up to date with events in the investigation and stay one step ahead of the law. He told the inquisitive newsagent that he had just come from the Highlands and was due to return there shortly. The newsagent was suspicious about what this man with a French-sounding name had been doing there. Then he recognized the resemblance between this Frenchman and the description given in the newspapers all around him of the fugitive American bank fraudster, George Bidwell. He discussed his suspicions with one of his customers, an employee of Messrs Gibson Craig, Dalziel and Brodie, the legal agents for the Bank of England in Edinburgh. This man, in turn, informed his employers about what the newsagent had told him. Although they probably doubted the validity of the report, Bank of England officials decided to play safe and engage a local detective called James McKelvie to make some enquiries into the matter.

At first the experienced investigator was not convinced by the story. He did not even visit the newsagent, instead deciding to make some general inquiries in Edinburgh. These inquiries turned up nothing and he finally interviewed the newsagent, probably just to put the matter to rest. McKelvie got some more details from the man and then, on Wednesday 2 April 1873, accompanied by a plain-clothes constable called McNab who had been requested by the clients, he visited the lodgings of 'Mr Coutant' on Cumberland Street. What they heard from the landlady, Mrs Laverock, may well have persuaded them to put aside their scepticism for a while: from what she said her lodger was of a similar description to George Bidwell all right. She told them that Mr Coutant had come from the Continent and was in 'rather bad health', and he had asked her to keep things as quiet as possible around the house. McKelvie and McNab decided to hang around for a while and take a look at this mysterious man for themselves. McKelvie asked Mrs Laverock not to tell the man that they were there, as he was probably not the man that they were seeking and there was no need to disturb a sick man unnecessarily. With that, they hid themselves at the bottom of the stairs to await the man's appearance.

Before half past ten, George appeared at the door and McKelvie got a nod from the landlady, who was stationed at a window in order to confirm his identification as the man in question. Contrary to what he had felt before, McKelvie now believed from the man's appearance and actions that he really could be the infamous George Bidwell. The man was acting very suspiciously, looking up and down the street a number of times before leaving the house. McKelvie remarked to McNab that these actions 'scarcely seemed like that of an honest man'.[1] When George left the house, they followed him to the top of Scotland Street and watched him post a letter. Then he walked on to Broughton Street where he bought some newspapers, followed by a visit to a baker's. Suddenly, George realized that he was being followed and took a number of sharp turns up various alleys in an attempt to lose his pursuers. When he was unable to shake them off, he began to run. His escape route led him to climb over a number of walls and the railings of a churchyard and at one point he actually ran through someone's house. He entered a blacksmith's shop but, finding that it was a dead end, had to re-emerge. As they ran, McNab got left behind.

When George realized that he could not shake off the dogged McKelvie, he suddenly changed tactics, turned on him and tried to hit him several times with his stick. The detective had been in perilous situations before and was not about to give up:

He made several thrusts at me with a stick he carried. I took a small bottle from my pocket and held it towards him, as though it was a pistol. I told him to stand and be a gentleman and give me his hand, and to be 'a brother' and not a coward. I seized his hand and stuck to it.[2]

For a moment McKelvie thought George was attempting to indicate to him that he was a fellow Freemason:

> I had fancied he gave me a Masonic sign and that was why I called him a brother.[3]

The tenacious McKelvie called a nearby coal porter to assist him with the arrest of the fugitive and George was finally subdued by the two men. When McKelvie said to him, 'You are George Bidwell, and you are wanted for the forgeries on the Bank of England,' he replied in what the detective described as 'French or some other language'.[4] All McKelvie could understand was that he was denying being a Fenian. The detective told him that he was aware of that and anyway he 'was not looking for Fenians'.[5]

George was placed in a cab and transported to the offices of McKelvie's clients, Messrs Gibson Craig, Dalziel and Brodie in Thistle Street. McKelvie had some time alone with him as they waited for the police to arrive:

> ... I asked him to account for his running over the private grounds and stone walls, but he made no answer. A few minutes afterwards he said he was subject to giddiness in the head, and took those sorts of fits of running off. He gave no name, and I asked him what I might call him. He answered, 'You may call me James if you like.' He spoke very broken English, like a Frenchman. He asked for a book to read, and I gave him one and he sat down. He said his father and his mother belonged, the one to France and the other to Germany, and that he had recently been in Paris.[6]

George's hands and legs were cut so badly from his determined attempt to escape that McKelvie had to get a handkerchief in order to 'bound up the wounds'. George complimented him on being a gentleman for his kindness. According to McKelvie it was two hours from the time of his arrest until George was finally taken by the police to their central office in the High Street. Even though he was still denying that he was George Bidwell, it was noticed that he was wearing sleeve links engraved with the initials 'G.B.'.[7]

Later that same day, David Ferguson, an Edinburgh city police detective officer, searched George Bidwell's lodgings at 22 Cumberland Street and a number of items were recovered: various items of jewellery including a number of watches and diamonds; a small amount of money; two Brazilian banknotes inside a pocket book with some other papers; a piece from a newspaper in which was listed the sailing times of ships. They also found a slip of paper inside an envelope addressed to 'Mr Joseph B. Bidwell, attorney, &c., South Bend, Indiana, U.S.A.', on which was written: 'There is a letter addressed to my wife's maiden name in full at your post-office, get and open it.'[8] In addition, there was a telegraph slip informing George that there was a telegram for him to collect at the post office.[9] When the police collected that telegram it said 'that the Alabama sailed on Wednesday morning, and he was to telegraph in reply if he wished to secure a berth, nine guineas being the charge for the cabin and six guineas for the steerage'.[10] Ten diamonds found at his lodgings were later valued by a jeweller in Edinburgh and found to be worth £150 each.[11] The reply to his request for accommodation in London from the landlady, Mrs Ann Thomas, addressed to 'Mr Anthony', was also found on his person when he was arrested.[12]

Even though he refused to give a name, the authorities felt confident that they had captured George Bidwell. An appearance at the police court followed on Thursday 3 April 1873. Detective Sergeants Spittle and Smith had travelled up from London armed with a warrant from the Lord Mayor. They saw George at the police station and Spittle read him the contents of the warrant, which charged him with defrauding the Bank of England. Still attempting to fool them, George answered the charge in broken English with a French accent, saying, 'Are you sure there is nothing political about it?' Spittle assured him that there was not and one of the Edinburgh police told him that it referred to a criminal charge. All of the material evidence that had been collected by the police in Edinburgh was handed over to the policemen from London.

The London policemen had brought two witnesses with them to identify the suspect. An employee of the shop Parkins & Gotto in Oxford Street, London, identified George as the man who 'had purchased a large number of travelling bags' from them. Mr Alfred Lidington, from Messrs Clews, Habicht and Co., the American bankers in London, gave evidence that the suspect had passed bills for discount and also bought bonds from them.[13] They, of course, had been suspicious of him at the time when he had refused to give a specific address.

George was transported to Waverley Station for the trip to London. On the way, according to Detective Sergeant Smith, he commented: 'I was very foolish; I ought to have faced it out at first.'[14] Such was the interest in the case that a large crowd had gathered at the station in Edinburgh to catch a glimpse of one of those responsible for the Great Fraud on the Bank of England. George wore 'an "Ulster" overcoat and a block "billycock" hat'. He looked sickly and walked with a limp, a consequence of his attempted escape from Mr McKelvie. A first-class train carriage had been reserved for his transportation to London and a large amount of luggage travelled with him, in which was carried his 'wearing apparel'.[15] During the train journey, according to Detective Sergeant Spittle, he made the comment: 'The man Noyes, who is in custody, is, I suppose, a person whom I knew as Howe, and who was introduced to me in that name.' The policemen had made no reference to Mr Noyes at all up to that point, but George said that he had got the information from the newspapers.[16] Detective Sergeant Smith read him a list of the property that had been discovered at his lodgings in Scotland and he confirmed that it was all his, including the ten diamonds. When George enquired about the rest of his property, he was asked if he meant the items that had been in Nelly Vernon's possession in London. When he replied yes, Spittle told him that they left Nelly the items that she claimed to be her property and only took the rest.[17] When he asked Spittle how many boxes and trunks there were, the policeman told him that he could not remember.

'Are you a naturalized American?' Sergeant Spittle asked him.

'Excuse me, I would rather not answer questions,' George replied.

'Very well,' said Spittle.[18]

The train arrived at Euston Station in London at around 9.30 p.m. and George was then taken by cab to Bow Lane police station. On the way, George asked Spittle if he could have his dressing case returned to him 'As it might be useful'.[19] The request was denied.

The prisoner was of such importance that the Assistant Commissioner of Police arrived at the police station to observe his questioning by Knight, the inspector on duty. George was asked to give his name on a number of occasions but, 'smiling slightly', he refused to do so.[20] He did give his address as Cumberland Street in Edinburgh but said 'he could not recollect the number'.[21] His profession he described as 'mercantile'.[22] When he was asked if that meant he was a merchant, he replied 'yes' but that he was 'out of business'.[23] According to Detective Sergeant Spittle, George asked for a solicitor and continued to refuse to answer questions.[24] Spittle noticed something about his accent: 'In Edinburgh he spoke like a Frenchman, but afterwards he spoke with an ordinary American accent.[25] He spent that night in one of the cells at the police station and was permitted to use one of the rugs from his luggage for comfort.[26] He was told that he would be taken to appear before the Lord Mayor in the morning.

CHAPTER 23

The New Prisoner

————•◦•————

W hile the others had been attempting to evade the reach of the law in places like Havana, New York and Edinburgh, Noyes, of course, was still very much within its clutches. He was being taken repeatedly from the deprivations of Newgate Prison to the much more salubrious surroundings of the Mansion House. For the first time, on Friday 4 April 1873, Noyes had one of the other suspects standing in the dock beside him. When asked his name, George refused to give it. He was permitted to sit down as a result of the injuries that he had suffered during his capture in Scotland. George's solicitor, Mr Lewis, had not yet arrived at court owing to the late notice that he had received and, when he did finally arrive, he explained to the Lord Mayor that 'he had been only just instructed on behalf of the new prisoner, and he should prefer not to discuss any of the matters in issue that day'.[1]

Mr Poland, when called upon to speak, asserted that the man sitting beside Mr Noyes was George Bidwell, 'whose name had been already adduced before the Lord Mayor'.[2] He was also able to confirm that 'there were, therefore, now four persons in custody in connection with this Great Fraud on the Bank of England – namely, Austin Bidwell, George Macdonnell, George Bidwell, brother of Austin, and Edwin Noyes.'[3] Although, of course, two of them were not yet back in England.

Mr Poland's main focus, he said, would be upon proving that the new arrival in the dock was George Bidwell, and on making the case for the gentleman's remand. With this in mind he called James McKelvie, the private detective from Edinburgh, so that he could testify regarding his arrest of George Bidwell in that city. McKelvie's account included a description of how George had tried to escape by running and how, when apprehended, he had pretended to be a Frenchman. Detective Sergeants William Smith and John Spittle were also called and gave evidence of travelling to Scotland in order to transport Mr Bidwell back to London. They described their first meeting with the prisoner, his answers to their questions and their journey back to London by train. Introduced into evidence was the confiscated personal property of George Bidwell that had been handed over to the London police by their colleagues in Scotland.

A number of other witnesses followed, all of whom were asked to confirm the identity of the new prisoner. Dr Kenealy once again objected to the continuing remand of his client, Mr Noyes, saying that this had been done six times now and he doubted 'whether the Lord Mayor, in his experience as a magistrate, ever knew of a prisoner being remanded six times'.[4] He had certainly never come across such a situation before himself. Mr Noyes, he pointed out, had been in custody since 1 March. He claimed that 'the Bank of England was trading on its character in asking the Bench to do what no private prosecutor would venture to ask'.[5] In the meantime, his client, being 'a stranger in this country', was 'entirely separated from his friends', and apart from some money coming to him from friends in America was bereft of any financial means with which to defend himself.[6] The real reason for all these delays, he said, was that Mr Poland had no evidence against his client. Furthermore, he argued that apart from newspaper reports there was no real evidence that the two other suspects in this case were even in custody. In any event, Dr Kenealy told the Lord Mayor, even if they were in custody, he doubted that they would ever be extradited back to London:

… the American authorities would never give up an American citizen unless there was sufficient evidence against him; and he challenged his learned friend to say there was a reasonable belief that Macdonnell and Warren would be brought here to answer the charge of forgery or conspiracy.[7]

Mr Poland, in response, quipped that Dr Kenealy's own presence in court was proof that 'the prisoner Noyes had not so far suffered

for want of funds, seeing that he had been from the first ably represented by a Queen's counsel'.[8] Poland claimed that Dr Kenealy's
real motive in wanting the inquiry expedited was 'to send Noyes
for trial alone, before the Bench had all the rest of the parties
supposed to be implicated before it'.[9] Furthermore, 'He did not
think anybody but his learned friend would doubt that Austin
Bidwell or Macdonnell was in custody, the former at Havana and
the other at New York.'[10]

Mr Poland was, he said, familiar with other cases where a
defendant was remanded as many as twenty times. He argued that
there was *prima facie* evidence in this case that the prisoner was 'a
party to the conspiracy' and consequently continuing with his
remand was essential.[11] The Lord Mayor agreed:

> He had felt from the first that the charge under consideration
> was an offence against the commercial community of an
> almost unprecedented character – unprecedented in its circum-
> stances and complications, unprecedented in the capital in
> which it was committed, and unprecedented in the length of
> time occupied in its development and perpetration... . He
> believed the authorities both in this country and in America
> were equally desirous that the parties implicated in this great
> fraud should be discovered and punished ... As to the prisoner
> Noyes, it was evident that he was associated with Austin
> Bidwell, now in custody abroad, and that he was known to
> George Macdonnell, and to the prisoner who was supposed to
> be George Bidwell, though he chose to decline to give his
> name.[12]

Therefore, both Noyes and George were remanded again and
conveyed to Newgate Prison. Once George was incarcerated in a
cell, the gravity of the situation was not lost on him:

> I at last had reached that dread[ed] abode of which I had read
> so much; that place, the scene of so many horrors in the dim
> and misty past, whose history, extending over a period of eight
> hundred years – one long record of crime – had rendered the
> very name infamous.[13]

The following morning he had a visit from the governor of Newgate, Mr Jonas, who told him that for 'half a crown per day' he could have food brought in from a restaurant rather than eating the prison food. He also told him that arrangements had been made for a 'cot' to be brought into his cell to replace the usual hammock on which prisoners slept.[14] The services of a doctor were offered for his injuries which, for the present, he decided to decline. He was brought to the yard for exercise. All very kind but, without doubt, small comfort for the situation in which he found himself.

In the weeks that followed, Noyes and George were repeatedly brought back to the Mansion House as the examination on the Great Fraud on the Bank of England continued. Sessions were held on 10 April, 17 April, 25 April, 2 May, 10 May, 16 May and 22 May, during which time Mr Poland worked hard to show the connections between George and Noyes, between them both and the other two suspects yet to appear, and between them all and the fraud itself. During this time the public and the court officials began to get glimpses of George's true personality. On one occasion, just as the session had been adjourned for the day, George was being led away when he turned suddenly to Nelly Vernon, who was in court, blew her a kiss and called out: 'Tell the truth and shame the devil, Nelly.'[15] On 10 April he requested from the Lord Mayor that he be granted a portion of the £21 that had been in his possession when he was arrested in Scotland so that he could buy some food in prison. The Lord Mayor agreed to grant him £10 of it.

By the time they came to the session held on Thursday 17 April 1873, George had grown weary of the British legal system. One of the first events of the day was his direct address to the Lord Mayor in which he announced that Mr Lewis was no longer his legal representative. He had been persuaded by Noyes to change his legal representation over to Mr Howell. George soon realized that he did not like Howell and, as it happened, he would come to regard this as 'a fatal concession'.[16] Then he told the Lord Mayor that 'as the whole case would have to be gone into again when the other men were brought back to this country, it would be better that no further evidence should be taken until those persons arrived'.[17] He was, he said, prepared to be remanded until that time. The Lord Mayor rejected his rather impertinent advice saying that 'he could not vary the course which was now being taken'.[18]

On another day George's slightly prickly relationship with the Lord Mayor was on show again. This time George complained to the Lord Mayor about being shown to witnesses for identification purposes 'in a place downstairs'.[19] In such a circumstance it was obvious, he said, that he was a prisoner and they were 'bound to identify somebody who had been arrested'.[20] The Lord Mayor replied that 'the men referred to had no interest in stating what was untrue'.[21] After all, he said, 'the prisoner could interrogate them all, if he liked, as to the surrounding circumstances under which they saw him ...'. George objected that for the purposes of identification it would be fairer 'to have him put with other men, and if possible, men who were a little like him'.[22] When the Lord Mayor reminded him that 'any man guilty of perjury was liable to severe punishment', George asked 'how he was to prove it'.[23] Again the Lord Mayor referred to his right to cross-examine witnesses, but George persisted, saying 'he felt he was placed in a very unfair position by the course which was being pursued'.[24] The Lord Mayor told him that if he could point out any officer who he felt 'had dealt unfairly by him in introducing a stranger to him', the matter would be investigated and the person concerned remonstrated with. In the end, however, the Lord Mayor did concede the point that 'no one had any right to take a witness downstairs to see him'.[25] He said that Colonel Fraser, the City Commissioner of Police, was sitting right beside him and would deal with any such case. George, in reply, said that although 'the matter was as he had stated it ... he did not want to get anyone into trouble'.[26] The matter rested there.

George may have been making sense when he wanted the hearings suspended but, despite his wishes, they continued relentlessly over the following weeks and the witnesses kept coming, from police officers to hotel staff members, shop workers, bankers, printers and engravers. During all this time Noyes' legal team tried repeatedly to get him released from custody. After all, by the time of his appearance at the Mansion House on Thursday 22 May 1873, he had been in custody for almost three months and it did seem as if the procedure was being drawn out and slowed down simply in order to wait for the arrival of Austin and Mac. The fact that they would all, eventually, be sent forward for trial at the Old Bailey was to most people a foregone conclusion. By Friday 25 April the perfunctory nature of the proceedings and the idea that the authorities were playing for time had also got through to the general public:

> The public interest in the matter seemed to have flagged considerably since the last examination, for that part of the court allotted to mere spectators was nearly empty.[27]

Mr Poland must have sensed the growing impatience too, because he felt it necessary to reassure the Lord Mayor on 25 April that events were progressing well and before long both the remaining suspects would be back in London.[28]

CHAPTER 24

Mr Warren Back in England

On 27 May 1873, the ship carrying Austin Bidwell, the *Moselle*, arrived into Plymouth harbour. Along with Detective Sergeants Michael Hayden and William Green, Austin was accompanied by two of the Pinkerton men, Curtin and Perry. Inspector Wallace and Detective Sergeant William Moss from the city police in London met them from the ship. The officers had to push their way through the large crowd in order to get to a cab that was waiting to take Austin to the Duke of Cornwall Hotel beside the railway station. Later, when he was put on the train to London, another large crowd, estimated to be around 20,000 people, had gathered to get a glimpse of the famous fugitive. Interestingly, most of those present cheered loudly for him.

Austin's thoughts were melancholic in nature as he arrived back in London. He contemplated the world of London high society, of which he had so recently been a member and from which he was now excluded; a world that could be no better illustrated for him than by the special date in the equestrian racing calendar on which he had arrived:

Accompanied by my escort of six, I arrived in London one bright Spring morning, just as the mighty masses of that great Babylon were thronging in their thousands toward Epsom Downs, where on that day the Derby, that pivotal event in the English year, was to be run. All London was astir, and had put on holiday attire, while I, now a poor weed drifting to rot on Lethe's wharf, was on my way to Newgate.[1]

He spent his first night back in London at Bow Lane police station. On Wednesday 28 May 1873, Austin finally stood before the Lord Mayor in the justice room of the Mansion House and the newspaper correspondents were understandably excited by his arrival:

> He is supposed to be the person who ... opened the two banking accounts – one in the name of Frederick Albert Warren, at the Western Branch of the Bank of England in Burlington-gardens, and the other in that of C. J. Horton, at the Continental Bank in Lombard-street – through which forged bills to the amount of nearly 100,000*l*. in all were passed.[2]

This first appearance was not alongside his brother and Noyes, but on his own. He was described as being 'in the prime of life, over 6ft high, and prepossessing in appearance and manners'. His age was given as around twenty-seven.[3] 'He appeared,' *The Times* correspondent said, 'cool and self-possessed, without any appearance of bravado, and his manner to the Court was deferential'.[4] Mr William D. Freshfield, solicitor to the Bank of England, acknowledged the various roles played in Austin's arrest and extradition by the Spanish government, the representatives of the British government abroad and the 'detective officers of the City of London'.[5] William Green, the City of London detective, was called as a witness and asked about bringing the prisoner back to England:

> ... he, in company with Sergeant Michael Hayden and John Curtin, a detective officer from Chicago, arrived at 4 o'clock that morning in London from Havana, in charge of the prisoner. He produced the warrant authorizing the prisoner's apprehension, and under which he had brought him to England. He was given into custody of witness at Havana by the Spanish authorities and put on board an English vessel.

When the Lord Mayor asked Austin if he wished to put any questions to the officer, he declined.

Colonel Peregrine M. Francis was then called to give evidence. For the first time since the forgery had been revealed, Colonel Francis found himself looking directly at the man he had known as

Mr F.A. Warren; a man whom he had once liked and admired. Colonel Francis stated for the record that he, as an agent of the Bank of England, based at the Western branch in Burlington Gardens, knew the prisoner as Frederick Albert Warren. He explained, once again, how the prisoner had opened an account in that name at the branch in the previous May and used it until 28 February of the present year. In reply to the Lord Mayor, he confirmed that 'the prisoner was the person who signed the signature book of the bank at their Western Branch'.[6] Once again Austin was asked if he wished to ask the witness any questions. This time he replied that if Colonel Francis was to appear at the next examination he might like to ask him some questions at that time. The Lord Mayor discussed the procedure with him:

> The Lord Mayor explained to him that the evidence already given by Colonel Francis at a former examination and by the other witnesses against the two men already in custody would eventually be read to the prisoner at a subsequent stage of the proceedings, and he would then have opportunities of asking any questions he might desire to put.[7]

Austin accepted this and did not ask anything of Colonel Francis. Before the session came to a close he requested that the Lord Mayor order 'the transfer to his wife of the jewellery and clothing which had been taken from him and the small sum of money that belonged to him'. He was granted 5*l.* of the money 'for present necessities' and remanded until the following Friday when he would appear beside his brother and Noyes. He was then dispatched to Newgate Prison.

When Austin appeared beside Noyes and George at the Mansion House for the first time, on Friday 30 May 1873, Mr Poland thought it apt to begin by once again outlining the details of the case as he saw it. During his remarks he intimated that there was no longer any doubt at all about the involvement of Noyes in the crime:

> It was idle now, however, observed Mr Poland, to say a word about Noyes; seeing that Austin Bidwell was before the Court,

the farce of Noyes acting as a mere clerk in the transactions in question had exploded.[8]

He also pointed to what he perceived to be Austin's important role in the affair:

> ... when Austin Bidwell fled the country, probably the confederates lost the coolest head they had among them. Until then it was thought he was an American gentleman of means and position, and not the remotest suspicion rested upon him until he went away.[9]

These kind of comments, of course, were intended to elevate Austin's role in the fraud to a high level. A number of the chief witnesses were recalled to support the main points of the prosecution case.

The appearances at the Mansion House continued, as did the supply of witnesses. On Thursday 5 June 1873, in the crowded courtroom, it was noticed that, for the first time, a police constable was positioned between Austin and George with the aim, it was thought, 'of preventing all communication between them ...'.[10] They had, obviously, been seen trying to talk to each other.

Finally, on 17 June, the authorities were able to announce the news that they had been waiting for – Mr Macdonnell's arrival back in England was imminent:[11]

> ... it was stated that George Macdonnell, who was then on his way from America in custody of Detective Sergeant Webb, would probably arrive in London on Monday night ...[12]

CHAPTER 25

Conclusion at the Mansion House

M ac arrived in Liverpool in the custody of Detective
Sergeants Webb and Hancock on Tuesday 17 June. By that
evening he was in London. On the following day, Wednesday 18
June 1873, all four Americans accused of the Great Fraud on the
Bank of England stood side by side in the dock of the Mansion
House before Lord Mayor Waterlow. For these four men, who had
not long before enjoyed the most luxurious lifestyles that London
had to offer, the accommodation at Newgate Prison was quite a
change. Austin found it difficult:

> This iron system is as cruel as unphilosophical, for, pending
> trial, the inmates are more or less living in a perfect agony of
> mind, which drives many into insanity or to the verge of
> insanity, as it did me.[1]

All of London, it seemed, was anxious to get a first glance at Mac,
about whom they had heard so much during the preceding months.

> His long confinement and consequent anxiety seemed to have
> told much upon him, and he had a careworn look.[2]

As the hearing began, Mr Poland explained to the Lord Mayor
that the depositions taken from the witnesses in London had been
sent to New York and had been used to attain Mr Macdonnell's
return to England so that he now stood beside his colleagues.[3] Mr
Poland thanked the American authorities for their assistance with
the case.

A handwriting expert, Charles Chabot, was called and he declared a number of letters in the possession of the prosecution to be in the handwriting of George Bidwell:

> He [Chabot] said he had made as yet no diagrams of the points of resemblance between the admitted handwriting of George Bidwell and that alleged to be his in the letters to persons in America in different names, but he expressed his firm conviction that all the correspondence ... was written by one and the same person. The bad spelling traceable in many of the letters had in no degree influenced his opinion, but he had formed his judgement on the general character of the handwriting, and not on its specialities or details. He pointed out several peculiarities in the formation of capital letters, and added that he was now engaged upon a minute analysis of the handwriting.[4]

During the course of his evidence Mr Chabot read out the letter that had been written by Noyes to his brother in America in which he referred to his mother and father. The contents of this letter affected Noyes so much that 'he burst into tears, which he tried in vain to conceal, and sobbed like a child at the recital of a passage in which he rejoiced at the prospect of keeping the homestead together for the family'.[5]

At one point, lengthy legal argument ensued as a result of a petition made by the prisoners. They asked, through their legal advisors, 'that some portion of the money and bonds found upon them at the time of their arrest, and alleged to be part of the proceeds of the forgeries, should be handed over to them for the purpose of their defence'.[6] Mr Poland, of course, objected to this petition saying that they 'were not likely to be in any want of means for their defence, seeing that 10,000*l*., which the bank had not recovered, had been sent to a brother of the Bidwells in America.'[7] The Lord Mayor refused to grant them access to these funds, saying that it would be the job of 'a superior court' to determine 'what should become of the property found on the prisoners'.[8]

Finally, on Wednesday 2 July 1873, the final sitting of the Lord Mayor's inquiry into the Great Fraud on the Bank of England came to its conclusion. The Lord Mayor addressed the prisoners directly:

> Having heard the evidence, do you wish to say anything in answer to the charge? You are not obliged to say anything unless you desire to do so; but whatever you say will be taken down in writing, and may be given in evidence against you upon your trial. Do you desire to call any witnesses? If you do it must be done after you have made your own statements.[9]

Noyes answered that he had nothing to say, while the others said that 'they would reserve their defence'.[10] The Lord Mayor then, as expected, committed them for trial 'at the next Sessions of the Central Criminal Court'.[11]

The examination at the Mansion House had proven to be a long affair, with twenty-three appearances for Noyes who, after all, had been in custody since 1 March 1873. Over 100 witnesses had been called and the printed version of the evidence ran to 242 folio pages. The Lord Mayor, cognisant of this fact, attempted to excuse the long duration:

> He had done everything he could ... to bring the preliminary investigation to a close as rapidly as possible consistently with the due administration of justice, and at the same time allowing the prosecution every opportunity to bring forward the necessary witnesses. Some of the most important evidence, documentary and otherwise, had to come from America, and the last of it did not reach this country until Wednesday in last week. These were the reasons which had necessitated so many investigations in that court of the circumstances of one of the most complicated frauds which he, as a merchant of London, ever recollected to have occurred in that city.[12]

Of course, many believed that he had merely been doing the bidding of the Bank of England by stretching out the proceedings until all four suspects had arrived back in London and could be sent for trial together. The strain had taken its toll on Noyes who, according to the correspondent at *The Times*, looked 'worn and anxious' on his last appearance at the Mansion House.[13] The same newspaper declared that, while Macdonnell and Austin Bidwell sometimes displayed 'unseemly levity' towards the proceedings, Noyes was different: he always behaved in a manner entitling him to respect, apart from the crime with which he is charged'.[14] Although *The Times* recounted that George Bidwell had behaved himself well before the Lord Mayor, this first taste of British jurisprudence had not been any joy for him:[15]

> Pilloried in the dock day after day, exposed to the gaze of unsympathetic and curious crowds of people, who coldly speculated as to the result ... and endeavoured to penetrate, by dint of staring, through the cloak of impassability with which the prisoner attempts to hide his real feelings.[16]

Before proceedings came to a close, George made a final request of the Lord Mayor. He requested that he and Austin be allowed contact with each other while awaiting trial. He made a passionate plea:

> He had now been three months in Newgate, undergoing the most rigorous solitary confinement, and on 16 or 17 occasions he had been pilloried in that dock. His position was greatly saddened by the fact that one who was so near and dear to him as his brother was should have been placed at his side on the same charge, and under circumstances which he desired to say were caused by himself alone. His brother was many years his junior, and, owing to family misfortune, he and several others were placed when quite young under his [George Bidwell's] charge. He found that, according to the rules of Newgate, two persons were sometimes allowed to occupy the same cell during some part of the day, and he asked that the privilege might be granted to him and his brother. He appealed to his Lordship, as himself a father, to afford them that last boon – that last gleam of sunshine which they might ever be permitted to enjoy, remembering that, in case of their conviction, they would be forever separated from each other, and would never meet again. It would be impossible for him long to survive the imprisonment which would follow a conviction.[17]

Austin added his voice to his brother's request by saying that what they wanted was that 'previous to their trial they might be allowed to be in each other's company at times, according to the rules of the prison, so that they might have an opportunity of preparing their defence and talking over family matters'.[18] The Lord Mayor informed them that such matters were not within his power to grant and the request would have to be made instead to the visiting justices for that month. He said that he would, however, 'take an opportunity of bringing the request before them'.[19]

Noyes then asked whether a ring that had been taken from him by the police might be returned. It was a small ring, he told the Lord Mayor, that had been a gift from his sister. He had not asked for it before now, he said, as he had never expected to be sent for trial.[20] The Lord Mayor gave instructions for it to be returned to him.

The four Americans were then removed from the Mansion House and transported back to Newgate Prison. The witnesses who had appeared at the inquiry were informed that they would be obliged, if asked, to give evidence once again at the forthcoming trial at the Old Bailey. With that, the spectacle at the Mansion House, which had been a sensation in London for months, was finally over:

> Within living memory there has been no such case, for length and importance, heard before any Lord Mayor of London in its preliminary stage, nor one which excited a greater amount of public interest from first to last.[21]

The authorities at the Bank of England would not be wrong in thinking that they had made great progress towards getting justice served against those who had wronged them. Having all the suspects now in custody and awaiting trial, as well as having two of them extradited back to England from overseas, was a great achievement. They were also determined to get as much of their money back as they could. With this in mind, on 27 June 1873 litigation commenced at the Vice-Chancellors' Courts regarding 'certain bonds, alleged to have been purchased by ... Austin Biron Bidwell, with the proceeds of certain forged bills of exchange'.[22] These bonds had been given to Austin's wife and the bank officials wanted them. She had given them into the safekeeping of a M

Stephen Philpot Low, who was a member of the firm of Grindlay and Co., described as East India agents and bankers.[23] Mr Low, under pressure from the Bank of England, refused to give the bonds up to Mrs Bidwell when requested to so do and legal proceedings were commenced against him in the name of Austin Bidwell. Mr Low then followed normal legal procedure by issuing 'an interpleader summons' which, in effect, required the Bank of England to back up their claim to the bonds:

> ... the Bank claimed to be entitled to the two bonds in question. Bidwell, on the other hand, denied the plaintiff's title and claimed the bonds as his own.[24]

The vice-chancellor granted the application made by the legal representatives of the bank to freeze the funds:

> [He granted] ... an interim order that the defendant Bidwell might be restrained from prosecuting the action, and from commencing any other proceedings for obtaining possession of the bonds; and also that the defendant Mr. Low might be restrained from proceeding with the interpleader summons and from delivering the bonds to the defendant Bidwell, or dealing with them in any manner without the plaintiff's consent.[25]

A further order was made at the same court, on 3 July 1873, to extend the original judgement.

> ... the Vice-Chancellor directed that the interim order should be continued till after this day fortnight. The motion to stand over, and special examiner to be appointed to take Bidwell's examination.[26]

On 17 July 1873, the following order was made regarding this matter once again, tying up the funds for the time being:

> That the defendant, Bidwell, should be restrained by injunction till the hearing or further order from prosecuting the action which he had brought against Mr. Low, of the firm of Grindlay

and Co., for the delivery of the bonds in question (which had been placed in his custody), and from commencing or prosecuting any other action to obtain possession of the bonds; and that Mr. Low should be restrained from proceeding with the interpleader summons which he had issued, and should be ordered to deposit the bonds in court to abide the decision of the Court, the bank to pay his costs both at law and in Chancery, without prejudice to the question by whom such costs should ultimately be paid, and to dismiss him from the suit.[27]

This was just one of a number of financial cases that demonstrated the Bank of England's determination to fight every battle on this issue no matter how small.

Meanwhile, the four defendants waited their fate at Newgate Prison. During his period of detention there, George claimed to have had a number of important visitors. He said that he was visited by Alfred de Rothschild. In the course of their conversation George said to him:

> Mr Rothschild, I believe most other men placed in the same circumstances, would have done much as I have. I was brought up honestly, and the greater part of my life I have been an honest man. I have plunged myself into a gulf of misery and degradation, but mark my words, I shall live to redeem my character, and, if force of will counts for anything, I shall not die until that end is accomplished.[28]

George asked him if he could do anything to help Noyes and his brother who, he said, were only suffering because of their connection to Mac and himself.[29] It became obvious to George, however, that Alfred de Rothschild had little respect for him:

> Having been protected from birth against every rough wind, Mr Alfred de Rothschild could see nothing in me worth saving, and the future will decide if he was right.[30]

He also claimed to have been visited by Lord Mayor Waterlow. George would later tell the story of how, when he went to his pocket to get something out, the Lord Mayor thought that he was going to assassinate him.[31] The Lord Mayor, according to George, was not too afraid to visit him again. He came back in the company of 'the Russian Prince Imperial'. Afterwards George would claim jokingly that 'I think I am entitled to call him an old friend, and to visit him at my earliest convenience in St Petersburg'.[32]

CHAPTER 26

Grand Jury

———•◦•———

The four Americans accused of the Great Fraud on the Bank of England were among forty-four prisoners whose cases were listed as part of the calendar at the July sessions of the Central Criminal Court when it met on 7 July 1873.[1] The next step in the procedure of the English justice system was a presentation of the details of the case before the Grand Jury. This was the final step between the prisoners and a full trial; the Grand Jury would listen to the details of the case and make that final decision. It was the responsibility of the deputy recorder, Sir Thomas Chambers, to outline the main points of the case for the members of the Grand Jury. He began by explaining the activities of the forgers at the Bank of England:

> On the 28th of February … the Deputy Chief Cashier of the Bank of England discovered that some bills which had been discounted at the western branch of the Bank bore forged acceptances, and on going next day to a banking-house in the City to make inquiries he found the prisoner Noyes, and gave him into custody. It afterwards turned out that no less than 92 bills had been discounted, each bearing the forged signatures of the alleged drawer and acceptor, and each being dated at a different place at home or abroad. The prisoner Austin Bidwell had, in May, 1872, opened a banking account at the western branch in the false name of F. A. Warren, and at the end of last year he gave out that he was going to leave London for Birmingham, where he was about to open extensive work-shops for the manufacture of railway sleeping-cars. His

account into which considerable sums had been paid and with-drawn from time to time, ran on until the 21st of January, ... He had previously induced the Bank authorities to discount for him bills which proved to be genuine ... and between that date and the 28th of February he transmitted from Birmingham for discount, bills to the extent of upwards of 102,000*l.*, all of which, as was subsequently discovered, were forgeries. There was no doubt whatever that they came from Austin Bidwell, for on that point there was most overwhelming evidence.

Then he went on to explain how the other account, at the Continental Bank, was used in the scam and what other strategies they had used to hide the stolen money:

During the whole of the five or six weeks in which the bills were being sent up, sums to the full extent of the discount were withdrawn by Warren from the western branch, and paid into another account which he had opened in the name of C. J. Horton, at the Continental Bank in Lombard-street. From that bank also they were gradually withdrawn, and after the bank-notes passed in payment for the checks had been changed into gold by Noyes, and the gold so obtained had been exchanged for other notes by Macdonnell, the money was expended in the purchase of United States bonds, which were forthwith despatched to America.

He made it clear how each member of the gang was involved:

Austin Bidwell, when the frauds were discovered, escaped to Havana, and from the evidence which had been brought forward against him, there could not be the smallest doubt that he was a party to the transactions. The prisoner Noyes, who had travelled in the name of Hills, arrived in this country in December last, and put himself in communication with the other prisoners. On the 11th of January a formal agreement was drawn up between him and Horton (Austin Bidwell), by which he agreed to act as Horton's clerk, and paid him a deposit of 300*l.*... . Noyes was introduced to the authorities at the Continental Bank by Horton as his confidential servant. Some evidence had been given to show that Noyes, so far from being a servant, was much more intimately associated with the other men, and it was alleged that the agreement was drawn up for the mere purpose of deception in case of the sudden discovery of the fraud. As to the preparation of the forged bills it was shown beyond all doubt that George Bidwell and Macdonnell had, in false names, gone over and over again to various printers and engravers in the City in December, January, and February last, and ordered certain blocks for acceptances, endorsements, dates, and names of cities all over the world, and that impressions of the stamps and blocks appeared on the bills in question.

He left his listeners in no doubt that this was a devilishly well-organized scam:

> The evidence disclosed one of the most elaborate conspiracies and gigantic frauds which had been heard of in modern times, and a good deal of it went to trace the various efforts which had been made to divert suspicion, and to prevent any clue being furnished as to the circumstances of the transactions ...'

The deputy recorder concluded his statement by saying that he expected the Grand Jury to 'return true bills against the prisoners'.[2] As expected, only a few hours later, the Grand July found sixteen true bills against the Americans, which meant that they would now stand trial before a judge. On the following day, 8 July 1873, they were 'placed at the bar' of the Central Criminal Court and arraigned on the various charges. They were asked to plead and they all pleaded not guilty to each charge, although George would later claim that he had wanted to plead guilty. Some of the experienced warders at Newgate had advised him that if he pleaded guilty the most he could expect would be a sentence of perhaps seven years. He was, he claimed, persuaded by his legal team to plead not guilty instead. He mostly blamed his solicitor, Mr Howell, for this decision.[3]

The trial was scheduled to take place during the August

sessions. Mr Metcalfe QC, who was representing Austin, requested that a proportion of his client's money, which had been confiscated, be returned to him to pay for his defence. He claimed that there was £10,000 of his client's money at the Bank of England which had nothing at all to do with the fraud. He also referred to the two bonds about which there was a dispute. These were two bonds, he said, that Mr Austin Bidwell had brought with him from America 'before the frauds were perpetuated'.[4] Austin Bidwell had given these to his wife to pay for his defence, but they were now held 'in the possession of Mr Low'[5]. Mr Metcalfe concluded:

> ... in justice to that prisoner, and in order that he might be enabled fairly to conduct his defence, some portion of the money in question should be given up to him by the prosecution ... without such restitution, the prisoner was absolutely destitute for the purposes of his defence.[6]

In a similar fashion, George Bidwell's legal counsel argued that his client should be given back £250. Macdonnell's also argued for the return of £22 that was on his person when he was arrested. The deputy recorder gave his opinion:

> ... it was quite true that the balance to the credit of Austin Bidwell at the Western Branch at the end of last year, and before any of the forgeries had been committed, was 3,600*l.*, but on the 21st of January, when the first batch of forged bills arrived, that balance had been reduced to 46*l.* The proceeds of those bills, amounting in the whole to 102,000*l.*, were added from time to time to his account, and subsequently withdrawn, and when the forgeries were discovered there was a balance to his credit of 1,859*l.* Inasmuch as it was impossible to earmark money, it could not be ascertained which part of that balance, if any, was honestly come by, and which had been obtained by means of the forgeries. Applications such as had been made by the prisoner's counsel were very common in that court, and were for the most part granted. The main question was whether the money or goods had been the proceeds of the

alleged offence, and if they were it would not be right to hand them over. Another point was whether or not they were necessary to be produced as links in the chain of evidence, and if so it was the practice not to accede to the application.[7]

Yet he was aware that the prisoners' defence would have to be paid for and that this case was 'of enormous public interest'.[8] In his opinion the case was a special one:

> ... it would be a discredit to the administration of justice that, in a case of that magnitude, the prisoners should be undefended, and he was, therefore, inclined, without going into the question of whether or not the money was part of the proceeds of the forgeries, to grant them a reasonable sum for the purposes of their defence.[9]

He granted the prisoners £100 each, out of the money held by the police, to pay for their defence.[10]

CHAPTER 27

Trial at the Old Bailey

———◆———

The trial began at the Old Bailey on Monday 18 August and ran for eight days until Tuesday 26 August, with Sunday off. There was still great interest in the case:

> The court-room of the Old Bailey was packed … the lobbies were filled and a crowd in the street waiting in the hope of eventually obtaining admission. Many of the nobility and gentry were present.[1]

It was well known that the depositions taken by Mr Oke at the Mansion House amounted to a substantial document of more than 242 pages, and this time even more witnesses had been identified and would be called to give evidence. On the opening day, the presiding judge, Sir Thomas Dickson Archibald, entered the courtroom watched by a large attendance of the most powerful legal and political figures in the country. As *The Times* put it, 'The members of the Bar mustered in unusual force …'.[2] The prosecution team was led by Mr Hardinge Giffard, assisted by Mr Watkin Williams, Mr Poland, Mr H.D. Greene and Mr J.H. Crawford. Mr Powell and Mr Besley were responsible for defending George Bidwell. The solicitor Mr Howell had retained Mr McIntyre and Mr Moody to act on behalf of Austin Bidwell, and Mr Ribton and Mr Hollings on behalf of Noyes. Mac's solicitors, Messrs Wontner, had retained Mr Metcalfe and Mr Straight as counsel on his behalf.[3]

The first action of George's counsel, Mr Powell, was to apply for a postponement of the trial owing to the complications of the case and the number of witnesses that were to be called. He referred to the length of time that it had taken to hear the case at the Mansion House.[4] All those representing the defendants in court supported Mr Powell's application. After some consideration, Mr Justice Archibald rejected the application for postponement and ruled that the trial would begin immediately as scheduled. The clerk of arraigns, Mr Avory, addressed the court:

> ... the prisoners were severally indicted for forging and uttering, on the 17th of January last, a bill of exchange for 1,000*l*., purporting to be drawn by H. C. Streeter, of Valparaiso, and accepted by the London and Westminster Bank, with intent to defraud the Governor and Company of the Bank of England. In other counts, he said, they were charged in like manner with other forgeries, variously stated.'[5]

Right from the beginning Mr Giffard, who was leading on behalf of the prosecution, left no doubt regarding the magnitude of the crime in question, telling the jury that the amount of the fraud came to over £100,000 and that it was a crime 'for which they might seek in vain a parallel in the criminal annals of the country'.[6] The jury heard how the prisoners had been paid the discounted value of ninety-four bills of exchange by the Bank of England over a period of two months, all of which were forged documents. Mr Giffard's opening statement took up the whole of day one and at five o'clock the trial was adjourned for the evening.

Over the course of the days that followed, a collection of witnesses were called to give evidence: they included bank officials and representatives of numerous financial houses, policemen, the handwriting expert, the female companions of the defendants, merchants, hotel owners and their staff. Most of those called had already given evidence at the Mansion House. James McKelvie, the private detective from Edinburgh who had been responsible for the arrest of George Bidwell, had died by the time the trial at the Old Bailey began and his evidence given at the Mansion House had to be read out in court. Nelly Vernon was deemed to be so valuable a witness that she had 'been kept under the strictest observation of the police', for her own protection, from the time of her appearance at the Mansion House until she testified at the Old Bailey.[7]

As the presentation of evidence on behalf of the prosecution came to an end, Mr Giffard stated that following recent statute he had enquired of his colleagues appearing for the defence of the prisoners whether or not they wished to call witnesses and they had indicated to him that they did not. The prisoners, having pleaded not guilty, were not entitled to give evidence themselves. The defendants were, however, given the opportunity of making a statement to the court. Mac opted to do this and he used the opportunity to argue for Austin's acquittal; he claimed that Austin had nothing at all to do with the actual committal of the fraud. After all, Mac pointed out, he was not even in the country at the time. Mac claimed that following his accident in France, Austin had experienced somewhat of a spiritual reawakening and had expressed a desire to re-evaluate his life. Mac also contended strenuously the assertion made by the prosecution that the crime had been premeditated by the gang a long time prior to February 1873. The authorities at the Bank of England and their representatives had tried to claim that he and his friends had only come to the country in order to carry out the fraud. The prosecution were well aware, he said, that a premeditated and carefully planned crime of that type was more serious and would, most likely, earn a greater punishment in the event of a guilty verdict. This was why the assertion was being made. It was untrue, according to Mac. He and his colleagues had only stumbled upon the idea of the fraud by chance when he had gone to a bank to discount a genuine bill of exchange and noticed how lax the procedures were in England compared to the USA. Austin's opening of the account with the bank in May 1872, with the assistance of Mr Green the tailor, had been nothing more than a chance happening and was not part of any long-term plan. In fact, he said, their intention had always been to close that account as soon as possible. They left England for South America on 28 May 1872 and at that stage had no intention of returning. In the end, however, events did not turn out well for them in South America and they did return to England. According to Mac, a premeditated, long-term plan to defraud the Bank of England never existed.

In the light of Mac's comments, apart from a few short words, George opted to waive his right to speak, saying that it would amount to 'mere repetition'.[8] He did claim, however, that Noyes was never a full and trusted member of their gang and, in fact, only ever did what he was told.

Mr McIntyre spoke on behalf of his client, Austin Bidwell, and he put it to the jury that there was no proof that his client had forged any bills of exchange or was even aware of a fraud taking place in England. After all, when Austin Bidwell opened that account at the Burlington branch of the Bank of England in May 1872, there was no fraud taking place and from that time until he left the country all transactions carried out concerning the account were 'perfectly honest and honourable'.[9] Quite simply, his client was not guilty of any crime.

On behalf of Noyes, Mr Ribton argued that he should not be treated like the others in this case at all. He was, he said, nothing more than a servant of the others. They gave him instructions, which he followed. That was it. His job was merely to act as a clerk, withdraw money from the account at the Continental Bank and use the money to buy United States bonds and the like:

> Not a single fact had been proved which would lead to the belief that he was concerned in the forgery, but throughout the whole transaction he had been the innocent dupe of the other men.[10]

Mr Justice Archibald, in his summing-up statement, alluded to the fact that Macdonnell in his statement to the jury and George Bidwell by stating that he agreed with it 'had virtually admitted their guilt'.[11] He also warned the jury about the argument that was being put forward by the defence that two of the prisoners, namely Austin Bidwell and Edwin Noyes, were less responsible for the crime than the other two:

> If the jury were satisfied that there was common concert and understanding between the prisoners to forge the bill or its acceptance, they all would be as guilty as if each had traced the bill and uttered it with his own hand.... if the evidence laid

before the jury led them to the conclusion that all the prisoners were engaged in a conspiracy with a common design and scheme to effect a fraud or felony, which was in fact subsequently effected, and that each one of them was a party to it, and intended that it should be carried out, they would all be guilty.[12]

But, of course, on the other hand, he was duty-bound to admit:

If, however, they saw any just ground for making a distinction between their cases, or felt a reasonable conviction satisfactory to their own minds that any one of them was innocent, though the others were guilty, they should, of course, give the prisoners the benefit of the doubt.[13]

It was then time for the jury members to consider their verdict and they left the court room at around seven o'clock for that purpose.[14] Returning after only fifteen minutes of deliberation, the jury found all four defendants guilty. In response to a wave of excitement in court, the armed policemen moved in around the prisoners, forming a cordon.[15]

Each prisoner was once again afforded the opportunity of speaking, should they so wish. Austin said that he had nothing to say on his own behalf, although, he said, 'he might at such a time have referred to opportunities thrown away and talents wasted'.[16] Instead, he used the opportunity to make a statement that was quite remarkable and demonstrated that the relationship between himself and Colonel Francis had not been entirely a false one. He said that he wanted to 'take advantage of the only opportunity he would have to repair a wrong he had done to a gentleman then in Court and for which he was extremely sorry'.[17] He said that he was referring to Colonel Francis of the Bank of England who, he was aware, had been the subject of 'considerable criticism' concerning the fraud:

... speaking from his knowledge of the circumstances he would say that any other man in London, however able, had he been in the position of Colonel Francis, would have been deceived in the same way as he was.[18]

He was, he said, 'extremely and sincerely sorry' to have deceived the colonel in that manner and he hoped 'that as the years rolled on the colonel's resentment towards him would wear away'.[19]

Mac, when asked if he had anything to say, tried to assert the innocence of Noyes, but Mr Justice Archibald objected to this use of his opportunity to speak. Mac did manage to say that Noyes 'so far as any forgery was concerned … knew nothing of it, and had no idea that forgery was about to be perpetrated'.[20]

George, practical as ever, used his opportunity to state his concern about the fact that all his money was now in the control of the authorities and he was left with 'not a shilling in the world'.[21] He requested that any money he had brought with him from America and which was not, therefore, the proceeds of the fraud, be handed over to a person named by him. Mr Justice Archibald replied that his court could not deal with such matters. George then made a final plea for leniency on behalf of his brother who, he said, 'was a young man, and recently married', and Noyes, who 'had been kept in ignorance of the real state of affairs'.[22]

Noyes, for his part, also argued that he had not been informed about the fraud that had been taking place. He admitted that he was an old acquaintance of the other prisoners, but he was not privy to the details of this particular job. He asked that the judge, in his case, 'temper justice with mercy'.[23]

Mr Justice Archibald then passed sentence on the Americans and, in so doing, made his feelings clear:

> I can see no palliating or mitigating circumstances in your offence. You were not pressed by want; on the contrary, you appear to have embarked in this nefarious scheme a very considerable amount of money… . You were not ignorant or unable to contemplate the full effects of the crime you were committing. You were persons of education, so far, indeed, as I can apply that term to mere intellectual training, without any corresponding development of the moral sense. Some of you can speak several foreign languages, and all of you were acquainted with the banking and commercial business.[24]

He accused them of having damaged the atmosphere of trust in which business and financial transactions had taken place in Britain up to that time: 'It is not the least atrocious part of your crime that you have given a severe blow to that confidence which has been so long maintained and protected in this country.'[25] In these statements he was echoing the sentiments of those at the Bank of England. As he neared the end of his statement, it was becoming clear to anyone listening that the sentence would be severe: '... as I cannot conceive a worse case, I cannot perceive any reason for mitigating the sentence.'[26] In the end, they were all handed down the same sentence:

> ... each and all of you be kept in penal servitude for life; and, in addition to that sentence, I order that each of you shall pay one fourth of the costs of the prosecution.[27]

George, Austin, Mac and Noyes could barely believe what the judge had said. Their legal advisors and the warders in Newgate, who had experience in such matters, had told them to expect a custodial sentence of perhaps ten years. It was not, after all, a case of murder, but of fraud, a crime against property. It seems that even Mr Freshfield, the solicitor for the Bank of England, had told Mac's solicitor that they would be 'satisfied with a ten years sentence'.[28] A sentence of ten years for George would have been difficult enough to bear, but penal servitude for life was unconscionable. For Austin, even prior to hearing the severe sentence, the experience of being in court at the Old Bailey had been horrible enough:

> For eight mortal days the final trial dragged on, and there we were pilloried in that horrible dock – a spectacle for the staring throngs that flocked to see the young Americans who had found a pregnable spot in the impregnable Bank of England.
>
> The misery of those eight days! No language can describe it, nor would I undergo it again for the wealth of the world.[29]

Forcing them to pay the cost of the prosecution was a concession to the Bank of England's demand for financial reparation.

In a severe state of shock, the prisoners were removed from the courtroom. They managed to utter a few words to each other as they were led through a passageway. According to Austin, they made a hurried pact before they separated:

> As we halted there in the gloom we swore never to give in, however they might starve us, even grind us to powder, as we felt they would certainly try to do. We knew that in their anxiety about our souls they would be sure kindly to furnish each with a Bible, and we promised to read one chapter every day consecutively, and, while reading the same chapter at the same hour, think of the others.[30]

George and Austin managed to have one last brotherly embrace before they were led away.

CHAPTER 28

The Highest Penalty Admissible

———•·•———

The prisoners and their supporters may have thought that the sentences handed down were severe in the extreme, but many others did not agree. For example, a writer for *The Times* said:

> … they have been most justly sentenced by the Judge to the highest penalty admissible for their offence … [1]

One cabinet minister at the time dismissed the argument that theirs was a crime against property and not, for example, murder. He was reported as saying: 'They are too clever to let loose. An attack on the Bank of England is, in my opinion, worse than murder.'[2] Understandably, the authorities at the Bank of England, with the huge resources they had contributed to achieving the convictions, were also pleased with the outcome:

> At a general court of the Bank of England the Governor (Mr Greene), in referring to the conviction of the Bank forgers, acknowledged the assistance that had been received from the Foreign Office, the American and Spanish Ministers, and the Captain-General of Cuba. A vote of thanks was passed to the Messrs. Freshfield for their skilful conduct of the prosecution.[3]

So grateful were they for the help of the United States Postal Service that they presented the secretary to the postmaster, Mr Daniel Gillette, with an attractive watch as thanks for his assistance.[4] It was engraved with the inscription:

Presented by the Governor & Company of the Bank of England to D. G. Gillette in recognition of valuable services rendered.[5]

After all, the interception of the gang's letters to each other, and to family members, had been extremely helpful in the investigation.

One writer for the *Illustrated London News* thought the sentence was 'heavy' but nevertheless 'every way merited'.[6] He, like the judge, thought it relevant that the men 'were not poor, ignorant men, but that they had had plenty of money and education'.[7] He pointed to the quality of the writing in the letters that had been produced in evidence at court as proof of their education:

> One of the writers knew how to wax exceedingly sentimental at need, and in addressing persons of the other sex to decorate his appealing letters with all those graces of quotations from silly love-songs, and those gushes of sham pathos which adorn our cheap literature, and are supposed to be exceedingly effective with foolish women... . The same scribe, in writing to those whom he had reason to fear, proved himself an able master of the art of mingling cajolement with menace, and of using with excellent skill such scraps of law learning as he had picked up.[8]

The prisoners themselves were devastated with the outcome. They may have prepared themselves psychologically for a prison sentence, but not 'penal servitude for life'. For the first time in his life, George could barely cope:

> I sat down upon the wooden stool in my dismal cell, and, as I reflected upon the situation, the sense of relief I had experienced faded away, and despair took its place. My past life – my errors, my lost family, friends, country – all rushed through my mind, and overwhelmed me like a tumultuous flood. I felt that my life was ended, and that I could not bear to live to see the light of another day. I picked up a slate and wrote a farewell letter to my wife, and destroyed all letters and papers. I considered the sentence an unmerciful one and worse than death.[9]

He contemplated suicide: '... the first night after the sentence ... I felt that I could not endure life longer.'[10] He was convinced that one of the reasons that they had been treated so unfairly was that they were foreigners and had no influential friends in England.[11] Austin's opinion of their sentence was no less negative:

> ... the evidence was most weak, and had our trial taken place in America under the too liberal construction of our laws, undoubtedly we all would have escaped. But in England there is no court of criminal appeal, as with us, and when once the jury gives a verdict, that ends the matter. The result is that if judges are prejudiced, or want a man convicted, as in our case, he never escapes. The jury is always selected from the shop-keeping class, and they are horribly subservient to the aristocratic classes. They don't care for evidence – they simply watch the judge. If he smiles, the prisoner is innocent. If he frowns, then, of course, guilty.[12]

He too believed that their nationality had gone against them:

> It was simply this – because we were youngsters and Americans, and had successfully assaulted the fondly imagined impreg-nable Bank of England, and, worse still, had held up to the laughter of the whole world its red-tape idiotic management, for had the bank asked [for] so common a thing as a reference the fraud would have been made impossible.[13]

Austin pointed to other cases, which he felt were comparable, but had very different outcomes. In one instance the actual manager of a bank and three of its directors had committed fraud on their own institution. Even though the amount involved was very large and some of the depositors of the bank had committed suicide as a result of their loss, the culprits were not handed down life sentences:

> They were tried, convicted, and in being sentenced were told that, being men of high social position, the disgrace in itself was a severe punishment; therefore, he should take that fact

into consideration, and ended by sentencing two to eight months', one to twelve and one to fourteen months' imprisonment.[14]

Both George and Austin also blamed the legal representation that they had received. Most of their ire was directed at the solicitor, Mr Howell. George was vehement in his reaction to the man:

> ... it was only by accident that he got into so important a case, and it was easy to see that all the eminent counsel engaged showed a decided repugnance to coming in contact with him, even to receive his 'retainers,' and paltry ones they were. Some to whom he applied would not take the case from him ...[15]

George regretted that he had not kept Mr Lewis as his legal adviser: 'Mr Lewis would have guarded against the occurrences which caused us to get the life sentences.'[16] George also had a financial grievance with Howell. Their brother, John, had come to London with funds in order to help pay for their defence. He asked Howell to sell $4,000 worth of US bonds that he had brought with him for this purpose. According to George, even though Howell had received these funds, he still applied to the court for an allowance in order to conduct their defence. By claiming that he had not received any payment from George or Noyes, he managed to get the judge to order £100 for each of the four of them.[17] As Howell was involved with three of them he received a total of £300. Mac had his own solicitor. Then, according to George, to make matters worse Howell told the barristers who were working on the case that this was all the money he had been paid and he persuaded them 'to work almost for nothing'.[18]

In Austin's view Howell was 'a thoroughgoing, unprincipled rascal' and a waste of money:

> ... a small, spare, undersized man, with little beady eyes, light complexion, red hair, and stubby beard, and when he spoke it was with a thin reedy voice.[19]

From first to last he managed our case in exactly the way the prosecution would have desired. He bled us freely, and altogether we paid him nearly $10,000, and our defense by our eight lawyers – four Queen's Counsels and four barristers – was about the lamest and most idiotic possible.[20]

They also now realized that they may have underestimated the power and determination of the Bank of England to use them as an example to other would-be forgers. As Austin put it: 'None of us was prepared for the vindictive fury of the Bank of England – its power was all-potent with the Government.'[21]

Another development had occurred that may also have had an impact upon the outcome of the case. Their hopes of being treated with leniency had not been aided by the fact that during the trial a story emerged concerning a planned escape from Newgate Prison. The first thing that anyone knew about this was when midway through the trial the security arrangements in the courtroom were suddenly intensified:

Alderman Sir Thomas White, upon information he had received, gave strict orders to the police in attendance that one at least, if not two, of the doors in the immediate neighborhood of the dock, and leading from the floor of the court to an outer corridor, communicating in two directions with the open street, should be closed.[22]

Armed policemen were now on duty in the courtroom and security at Newgate Prison was strengthened: [23]

Six policemen, well armed, are now on duty within the gaol at night …; a vigilant watch, moreover, is kept outside and all round it day and night.[24]

It was claimed that an attempt had been made to bribe three warders at Newgate Prison with a view to facilitating the escape of the Americans. According to the story, George and Austin's brother, John Bidwell, along with Mac's cousin, had come over to London for the express purpose of arranging the escape and paying for it. John Bidwell had become a familiar figure to many people in court from his daily attendance at the trial. It was ordered that an immediate investigation be held into the matter. Attention soon became focused upon three prisoner warders. At least two of the warders were said to have received £100 each from either the prisoners or their relatives. It was reported that one warder had been observed talking to John Bidwell on board an omnibus and that he had received money from the American. It was also claimed that two of the warders had been seen fraternizing with relatives of the prisoners and that they met in a house owned by one of the warders in the East End of London. The escape, it was claimed, was arranged to take place on the Friday night of the week that the trial was on:

> It is a remarkable fact connected with the affair that all the three suspended warders would have been on duty in the prison during the night on which there is reason to believe that attempt to release the prisoners was to have been made.[25]

With the three warders suspended from their positions, George claimed that this report of a planned escape was nothing more than a 'tempest in a teapot'. He did admit that something had happened, but he put the blame for it on the warders. He said that these three characters had figured out that John Bidwell was 'of an honest, confiding nature, and believing he had money, they concluded to try for some of it'.[26] They suggested that they could, for a fee, get hold of copies of the cell keys. When George heard about the plan he thought it was a foolish idea that could not work; apart from anything else, their faces were too well known to the public by then. Also, he did not trust the warders to perform their part in the plan. At the very least, he said, the money would have to be paid into the hands of a third party and only released to the warders when the escape had taken place. George told his solicitor, Mr Howell, to dissuade John from enacting the plan, but by then John had already paid the warders the money. Mr Howell then went to the Governor of Newgate with the story and everything was exposed. Howell advised John Bidwell to flee the county, which he did.[27] His actions in all this only confirmed George's low opinion of him:

It was Solicitor Howell who gave Governor Jonas information, exaggerating something I said to him, thus causing the great scare during the trial about an alleged plan of escape.[28]

George was convinced that the whole debacle was a major contributing factor to the extremely harsh sentence that had been handed down to them.[29] Some years later even the judge's son believed that the atmosphere created by the rumours of a possible attempted escape had an effect on sentencing. He even admitted to George that the judge had come to court bearing arms:

> During the trial I sat beside my father, taking notes for him. Everyone believed a rescue would be attempted. That is why you were sentenced without a moment's delay after the jury had rendered the verdict of 'guilty.' Besides the swarms of officers in uniform and in citizen's dress, all officials, including the judge and officers of the court, were armed; and we all breathed a sigh of relief when the sentence of 'penal servitude for life' was passed and you four Americans were safe behind the bars of Newgate.[30]

Austin's young wife, Jane Georgina Mary Bidwell, decided to have no more to do with her husband after the conviction. She was only eighteen years old at the time and it now emerged that not only had she lost her new husband in terrible circumstances, but also suffered the loss of their baby daughter. In October 1873, at Bow Street Court, she was identified as the wife of the convict Austin Bidwell and accused of 'concealing the birth of her female child'.[31] A rather bizarre and sad story unfolded:

> ... about a week ago an undertaker in Vauxhall-walk, Lambeth, received by Parcels Delivery cart a box addressed to him. On opening it the box was found to contain the body of a female child.[32]

The police received an anonymous letter about the identity of the mother and on foot of that went to the lodgings in Oxford Street of Mrs Jane Bidwell and her mother Mrs Devereux. Mrs Devereux told the police that it was she who had sent the box to the under-taker in Lambeth. She was quite open about it: 'Yes, it is true,' she said. 'What was I to do with it?'[33] She told them what had happened:

> ... her daughter had met with an accident on board a boat a few weeks previously, and that, she believed, had brought on premature confinement. She had no doctor or friend, and wrapped the child up in a newspaper before placing it in the box. Subsequently, she said she had put 6s. in the box for the burial, and taken it to the booking office.[34]

The child had been born on 20 September and the post-mortem revealed no evidence of foul play. The box was described as 'a small wooden one, bearing the label 'Hudson's Extract of Soap'.[35] It was, undoubtedly, an attempt by Jane's mother to avoid yet further scandal and public linking of her daughter's name with her criminal husband's. At the hearing Austin's young wife 'appeared very ill' and was remanded to St Giles's Workhouse for a week, where she had already been under the care of a doctor.

At a subsequent hearing the undertaker said that the box had been delivered to him on 6 October 1873. It contained the body along with 'a towel, newspaper, and some bran', but, according to him, no money.[36] Mr Poland, on behalf of his client Mrs Bidwell, said that there was no evidence against her:

> ... It was shown that she was extremely ill when taken in charge. It was very possible that a girl so young as the prisoner would leave the charge of her first child in the hands of those whom she esteemed better able to take care of it.[37]

She was described as 'a well dressed woman, of respectable appear-ance'.[38] Another woman present in court, Catherine Bassett, was also implicated, when it was claimed by a parcel delivery company official that it was she who had actually brought the box to them. The case against all three was sent forward for trial at the Old Bailey.[39] In the end, on 25 November 1873, the case came to nothing when it was rejected by the Grand Jury and did not proceed to trial.[40] The members of the Grand Jury had obviously regarded the poor young woman, rather sensibly, as a victim and not a criminal. Jane did eventually remarry and Austin, when he heard about it, felt bitter:

> ... could I have foreseen that this woman, on whom I had settled a fortune, would have married another soon after my sentence, I should not have felt so sorrowful on her account.'[41]

It was a bitterness, no doubt, based on feelings of sadness and lost opportunity.

In the aftermath of the trial one issue to be settled was the destination of the reward money that had been put up by the Bank of England for information leading to the capture of the perpetrators of the crime. The decision regarding who was entitled to a reward was left to the Lord Mayor, Sir Sydney Waterlow, acting as referee on behalf of the Bank of England. He decided that among the chief recipients should be Miss Green, the owner of the hotel at St James's Place, who got £250 for information leading to the capture of George Bidwell and £200 for Mac. Mr Gardner, the operator of the news stand in Edinburgh who identified George, got £150 for his vigilance. The manager at Parkins & Gotto got £100, while Mr Jesse White got £150 for himself and his wife. There were also a number of other smaller rewards made of £50 each.

There was a legal dispute regarding some of the property that Mac had on him when arrested in New York. The items, valued at around $2,000, included a number of diamonds and two ladies' watches.[42] They were held by the authorities at the Custom House in New York waiting for some party to take possession of them and pay the outstanding duties. Both Mac's solicitors, to whom he had assigned them in payment of legal fees, and the Bank of England claimed an entitlement to the valuables. Once again the Bank of England won the day:

> The matter having been referred to the Treasury Department, the attorney of the United States at New York has been

instructed to begin suit for the confiscation of the articles, and the balance over the duties realized from the sale (if any) will be awarded by the Court to the Bank, as it evidently has a prior claim to the forger's counsel.[43]

CHAPTER 29

Like a Good Citizen

In the end, any hopes for a reversal of the sentences proved illusory. All appeals for leniency went unheeded and the four Americans began their long periods of incarceration in English prisons. As was the practice, they were all sent first to Pentonville Prison where they spent nine months in virtual solitude. George was only six months into his sentence when he was restrained by ankle 'bracelets' joined to each other by a chain, which he had to wear twenty-four hours a day for six months. This was to cause him lasting physical effects with regard to his mobility and ability to stand.[1] Following the nine months in Pentonville, George was moved to Dartmoor Prison. Many other deprivations followed during his long years behind bars:

> During the first five years of that period I was never out of the cell in which I was confined, except once a month to the bathroom in the ward. After the expiration of the five years, I was taken out into the yard for an hour each day. This continued for a month, after which I was again in the solitude of a cell for the space of two years.[2]

In 1874 Austin was moved from Pentonville to Chatham Prison where the governor, who Austin regarded as a pompous little man, told him bluntly: 'You were sent here to work, and you will have to do it or I will make you suffer for it.'[3] Austin noted the appearance of his new fellow inmates: '... their famished, wolfish looks – thin, gaunt and almost disguised out of all human resemblance by their ill-fitting, mud-covered garments and mud-splashed faces and hands.'[4] The governor had been speaking the truth – he did have to work there and in terrible conditions:

> Mud, mud everywhere, with groups of weary men with shovel, or shovel and barrow, working in it. A sort of road had been made over the mud with ashes and cinders ...[5]

Throughout their long years of captivity many important people on both sides of the Atlantic continued to campaign for their release. Much of this effort was orchestrated by the Bidwells' sister, Mrs Henrietta C. Mott, who worked tirelessly on their behalf for many years. It was to be a difficult struggle:

> Her first step, after it was resolved to undertake an active campaign, was to break up her home ... and prepare to move to London. Before crossing the ocean she enlisted a number of prominent persons in Washington and New York in her case, and then she sailed for London.
>
> Almost on the day she landed she opened her campaign. The Rev. Theodore L. Cuyler of Brooklyn and a number of other well-known Americans were in the English metropolis when she got there, and taking the Brooklyn clergyman into her confidence she prepared for a descent on the Home Secretary. Her plan was to surprise that functionary into an audience which, she knew, would never be granted if it was known to have the pardoning of a convict for its object. She therefore induced Dr. Cuyler to make an appointment with Mr. Mathews, who then held the Home Secretaryship, to 'meet a delegation of Americans'. Mr. Mathews readily made the appointment, but when the delegation, which had been so laboriously drummed up by Mrs. Mott, arrived, the Home Secretary sent out word that he would be unable to receive the visitors. Someone had apprised him of the object of the call.
>
> But this failure did not discourage the resolute woman. She began to haunt the Home Secretary's office until she became as well known there as any of the regular employees. She made friends among all the well-known philanthropists ... In this

way she gradually made an impression, but the Home Secretary still remained obdurate...[6]

In the end, it was a fortuitous transfer to Woking Prison that helped to facilitate George's release. He was first sent there in November 1881. The conditions at Woking were not any better than those he had experienced previously; in fact, following his transfer there, he was kept confined in his cell for a further three years.[7] The fortuitous element was that the move to Woking brought him into contact with one Dr Vane C. Clarke, whom he had previously known as the prison doctor at Pentonville. George had come to regard him as a person who was 'truly Christian'.[8] Even when George was at Pentonville, Dr Clarke had thought his physical condition warranted an early release. The doctor was now the governor at Woking and was in a position to assist in achieving his release:

> ... Dr. Clarke found, when the forger convict came under his charge at Woking, that his diagnosis, made thirteen or fourteen years before, had been correct, and he reported that unless Bidwell was released at once he would undoubtedly die in the prison within the next year or two.
> Upon his representation George Bidwell was granted his freedom by the Home Secretary ...[9]

So it was, after fourteen years of suffering in harsh English prisons, George finally got his freedom back. He was not granted a full pardon, but was released on a 'ticket of leave', under which convicts were freed as long as they abided by certain conditions. His release was dated 18 July 1887. One condition of George's release was very clear:

> ... by the terms of his pardon he was precluded from setting foot on English soil again under penalty of being reincarcerated ...[10]

George was aware that his physical condition had deteriorated significantly during his years of incarceration:

> Though I began those years a black-haired, robust young man, at the end I found myself a gray-headed cripple.[11]

The end of his prison life came quite quickly and without much ceremony. A prison official entered his cell around 1 p.m. and addressed him with the words:

> You are free! And I am going to London by next train with you! A dispatch has come that you are to be sent at once![12]

That was it. With those words his years of imprisonment were at an end. His convict's garb was removed and he was provided with civilian clothes. Once he had been given a routine medical exam, his photograph was taken and whatever other procedures were usually performed at such a time were attended to; then he was transported to the railway station by two prison warders. Along with the warders, who were also dressed in civilian clothes, he boarded the train for Liverpool. His watchers did not leave him until he was on board the steamer bound for America:

> The Government apparently feared that I, crippled as I was, might give them the slip and remain in England, and these officers were obliged to report that they saw me sail, and to bring a certificate signed by the captain to that effect.[13]

When the steamship *Wisconsin* paid its usual stopover visit to Queenstown in Ireland to pick up more passengers bound for America, George noticed a man come on board who he firmly believed to have been sent there by the government to keep an eye on him and make sure that he did not disembark. George's sister accompanied him on the trip home.

The ship docked at the Guion Line wharf in New York on 4 August 1887, and George was about to set foot on American soil for the first time in many years. His wife and son were there waiting to greet him. Any feelings of euphoria that he was feeling at the moment of arrival were soon dissipated when, even before he left the vessel, he was arrested by the New York police. He was taken by Detective Sergeants McGuire and Doyle to police headquarters in Mott Street under orders from Inspector Byrnes.[14] The detectives were surprised at how feeble he was as they had to support him in walking to their carriage. After some time, and with his family in understandable distress, he was transported to Jefferson Market Police Court to appear before Justice Duffy in a private room. However, on finding that the man before him had no warrant outstanding against him and no charges of any kind to answer, the judge expressed himself to be displeased with the action that had been taken by the police. The police explained that they had arrested him as a precautionary measure.[15] The judge informed them that their suspicion of someone being 'too dangerous' to be left at large was 'no ground or reason whatever for depriving a man of his liberty'.[16] He was aware, he told them, that George Bidwell had served fourteen years for a crime committed in a foreign country and had, therefore, paid the price:

> It would be against every principle of justice to interfere with him, so long as he conducts himself like a good citizen.[17]

George's reputation as a celebrity criminal and forger created considerable interest among the police:

> While at the Headquarters the detectives all scrutinized Bidwell closely in order to recognize him in case he should ever return to his old profession.[18]

Yet the consensus among those who saw him and spoke to him was that he no longer posed a criminal risk:

> ... there is little chance of his ever becoming dangerous again ... With tears in his eyes he said he had come here to put himself in the hands of his wife and redeem the past. He had caused his wife and son great sorrow, and now he would endeavour to repay them in a measure. His wife, he said, was a woman in ten thousand, and had acted a noble part toward him.[19]

George was free and he went home with his family, yet there could be no peace of mind for him while his brother was still in prison in England. He always believed that Austin was suffering because of illegal activities to which he had introduced him in the first place and he felt a lot of guilt about that. George began immediately to become involved with his sister, Mrs Mott, in campaigning for the release of Austin and the others. In 1887 a petition was sent to the Home Secretary supported by a number of important personages of the day such as John Bright MP, Randolph T. Churchill MP, Charles Russell QC and the American Ambassador to Britain, Edward John Phelps. The eminent petitioners requested that a review of Austin's case be conducted since, as the politician John Bright and others put it, 'A life sentence on a young man ... for an offense against property, seems ... very harsh and inconsistent with the better feeling prevailing in our time.'[20] This was followed, in early 1888, by the application of more pressure on the Home Office in the form of letters from the writers Harriet Beecher Stowe, Charles Dudley Warner and Mark Twain.[21] At first the Home Office resisted and none of the others were released. Yet Mrs Mott and George continued their campaign, now using George's release as a precedent:

> ... if the Government could release a man who had notoriously been the leader in the great crime, it ought certainly to grant the same clemency to the men who had been only the instruments for the carrying out of his plans. Austin Bidwell, who had been in Chatham Prison during all the intervening years, had been little more than a boy when the crime was committed, having just passed his twenty-fifth year. The life sentence imposed on him might mean forty years or more of imprisonment.
>
> Under this constant fire the British officers gradually became somewhat softened, but they still declined to consider the application for a pardon, on the ground that the sentence had been imposed deliberately by an English court after a fair trial by jury, and nothing had occurred to alter the facts adduced at the trial.[22]

George became very frustrated with Home Secretary Matthews attitude and was quoted, at one point, as having said: 'If I ha Secretary Matthews over in America I'd punch his nose for him.'[2]

Even the son of the trial judge felt that it was now right to review Austin's sentence. In fact, when petitioned by the Bidwells, he had some interesting comments to make on the original sentence:

> Were my father now alive and had the sentence to pronounce again, I do not believe it would be one of life for your brother and Noyes. I have no doubt, if alive, he would sign a petition for their release, which I am glad to do, and will aid your efforts for the release of your brother Austin to the best of my ability.[24]

Everything seemed to change when Austin, who had served eighteen years, saved a fellow inmate from drowning one day at Chatham as they were engaged in prison work dredging the river Medway.[25] A water pump gave way, hurling the unfortunate man into the water and Austin, without thinking, dived into the river and pulled him to safety. Mrs Mott made sure that the Home Secretary heard of the incident:

> Long before she [Mrs Mott] had given up all attempts to see Mr Matthews in person, but she had made friends of all the people in the office, and through them she managed to get the story of the rescue to the Home Secretary's ear.[26]

The act of kindness and bravery gave the authorities, and the Home Secretary in particular, the excuse that they felt was needed in order to review Austin's case. On consideration, his sentence was commuted to twenty years, of which eighteen months were remitted for good behaviour. This meant that he was released on a ticket of leave in 1892. He would never forget the moment when nineteen years of captivity finally came to an end and freedom beckoned at Chatham Prison:

> It was a frosty February night, and I was alone in that little room with its arched roof and stone floor. It was past 7 o'clock, and the prison gloom and stillness had settled down on all the inmates, when suddenly there came the noise of hurrying feet that echoed strangely from the arched roof as

the warders tramped loudly on the stone floor of the long hall. A rush of feet, or, indeed, anything that broke the horrible stillness at that hour, was startling. They were the feet of the reserve guard, which was never called in save when the patrol who glided around the corridors in slippered feet discovered some suicide. Many a heartbroken man had I known in that twenty years who in his despair ended his misery thus.

While wondering who the unfortunate could be I heard their steps mounting the stairway leading to my landing, and then a sudden thrill shot through me as they turned down the corridor toward my cell. My heart stood still as I thought, could they be coming for me? I had a sudden frenzy of fear that they might pass my door, but no, they came straight on, halted, and Ross, a principal officer – I had known him twenty years – gave a thundering rap on my door and shouted, 'I want you!' Then a key rattled in the lock, the door was thrown open and three friendly faces looked in. Faint, deadly white, trembling like a frightened child, I started to my feet trying to speak, but no sound came from my lips for a moment. At last I stammered, 'What's the matter?' Ross thrust his form through the door, and with face close to mine said the thrilling words, 'You're free!' I cried, 'I don't believe you!' and Ross said: 'Come on, my boy; it's all right.' '[27]

Austin's brother and sister were informed of the good news:

... the Home Secretary wrote ... that 'in consideration of the gallantry displayed by the convict, Austin Bidwell,' he should have his life sentence commuted to twenty years, from which eighteen months would be remitted for good behaviour.[28]

On 13 February 1892, Austin was met by his sister at the prison gate as a free man at last. He and his sister arrived back in the United States of America on 21 February:[29]

Austin Bidwell, one of the notorious quartet who ... forged notes and bills of exchange on the Bank of England ... stepped over the gangplank of the *Etruria* when that vessel reached her pier yesterday forenoon.[30]

Finally, in August 1892, the whole saga of the Great Fraud on the Bank of England was brought to a close when Mac and Noyes were granted their tickets of leave and released from prison. They too had to leave Britain and not return.[31]

CHAPTER 30

Life Afterwards

---·•·---

The tough years George and Austin had spent in prison were documented by them in their respective books and in the public lectures they gave around the country. As outsiders, they were able to give valuable contemporary accounts of the brutality, corruption, punishment and inhuman conditions that existed inside English prisons in the nineteenth century:

> Upon a large screen in Chickering Hall last night a stereopticon threw a facsimile of a Ticket-of-Leave granted by the English authorities on his release from prison to George Bidwell, the leader of the quartet of American forgers who robbed the Bank of England ... in 1873. It was granted after Bidwell had served fifteen years of a life sentence.
>
> Beside the screen stood Mr Bidwell, and for two hours he talked of his crime, the long chase he gave the detectives, his arrest, his trial, and his hardships in prison. Upon his left sat Austin Bidwell, his brother, who was with him in his crime and released from Chatham Prison about two weeks ago.
>
> ... George Bidwell is rather above medium height, and he has a large, round head and an honest-looking face. His hair is iron-grey and bushy, and he has a heavy iron-grey moustache. His hands are large and the fingers are bent out of shape. This, he said, was due to the tortures of the strait-jacket, which he had been forced to wear for days.
>
> ... The younger Bidwell is still thin from his prisoner life. Almost 6 feet in height and well proportioned, he weighs less than 130 pounds. His hair is coal black. His face is florid, and

black side whiskers hide his hollow cheeks. His voice is hoarse and rasping, and he has not yet gotten over his prison habit of talking without moving his lips. This, he said, was a habit all prisoners formed to escape the eye of the guard. His long association with Englishmen has given him a pronounced English accent.[1]

Towards the beginning of 1899, George and Austin decided to head west in order to pursue their business interests and continue their lecture and book tours. Some said that they had an interest in going into the mining industry.[2] Their time in the British penal system, however, had had a profound effect upon the health of both men. On 7 March 1899, while on this trip and only seven years after his release from prison, it was the younger brother who succumbed first to his physical frailties: in Butte Montana, Austin Bidwell died at the age of only fifty-two. *The New York Times* gave the cause of death as 'grip' and said that he had been sick for about a week.[3] This probably does not give much information about the exact cause of death, however, as *The New York Times* in 1900 described the ailment 'grip' as 'a convenient vehicle for attesting the inability of the doctor to specifically diagnosticate his patient's … symptoms'. Austin was remembered by the newspaper as 'one of the most remarkable criminals in his line of business that this country has produced'.[4]

Sadly, only a few weeks later, on 26 March, before Austin was even buried, George developed pneumonia and also died.[5] Perhaps the reporter was correct when he wrote: 'He was taken with pneumonia a week after the recent death of his brother, and his constitution proved unequal to the ordeal.'[6] Austin's death had been too much for him to bear. George Bidwell was sixty-six years of age.

Butte, Mont., March 27 – George Bidwell, the elder of the two brothers who gained worldwide notoriety by successful forgeries on the Bank of England in 1873, died in a lodging house here yesterday of pneumonia. He was ill two weeks. His brother, Austin Bidwell, died in the same room three weeks ago, and his body still lies unburied at a local undertaker's.

The death of Austin was a crushing blow to George, and for several days he acted so strangely that it was feared he would go insane. His mind wandered and he was affected by delusions before he was attacked by pneumonia... . The two Bidwells were greatly attached to each other. They came to Butte in the latter part of February with the intention of selling their book, but did not meet with success. The money never did any good to any of the forgers. Some of it was frittered away in riotous living. When George arrived in New York on his release from prison he was a very poor man, and he and Austin never had any money to speak of. They had relatives in Harford, Conn., who looked out for them. They made a little money at odd times going about the country lecturing on their experiences in English prisons.'[7]

Mac's life did not work out too well after his release from prison either. As specified by the terms of his release, he left England and returned to America. According to quotes that he had given to the press, he was 'determined to lead an honest life'.[8] But the ways of the swindler die hard. In September 1892 he announced to his friends that he was going to France, 'where he had money in a bank, placed there twenty years before'.[9] Not many were convinced by the story. Shortly afterwards, having heard nothing from him, his sister travelled there to see if everything was all right. Unfortunately, she found Mac once again incarcerated in prison. It transpired that he had run out of money in France and was faced with an unpaid hotel bill. He gave the owner of the hotel a cheque for the amount that he owed plus a $25 excess, which it seems he intended to use for his fare home to America. The cheque, of course, bounced and Mac found himself back behind bars. It sounded to Robert Pinkerton of the detective agency as if Mac may have been suffering from some degree of insanity by this time.[10]

As for Noyes, at the time of his release from prison he was described as being 'a white-haired man with his mind totally deranged'.[11] No doubt the long years in prison had an effect on him as well and he became a slave to gambling. Then in January 1897, it was reported that Mac and Noyes were back in trouble together in Chicago, where they may have been up to their old tricks.[12] They were accused of ordering 'a set of letterheads' in the name of the J.W. Butler Paper Company from a printers at Joliet. The printers became suspicious that some kind of forgery was afoot and both Mac and Noyes were arrested. The press did not miss the irony:

> Men who once stole millions are reduced to a pitiful attempt at petty swindling by forging letterheads! Such was the spectacle presented at the Central Station today when George Macdonnell and Edwin Noyes Hills were led toward dingy cells.
>
> Macdonnell and Hills, two of the men who robbed the Bank of England ... and who served long sentences for their crime, hung their heads and looked almost heartbroken.[13]

It was reported later that Mac was serving 'a short sentence' in California in 1905.[14] He died in San Francisco a few years later. It was Noyes who survived the longest. His 'ticket of leave' from the British penal system was cancelled in 1908 and he was, from then on, an officially free man.[15] When he paid a return visit to London in the same year, he was described by the newspapers as 'a brisk, alert old man ... with a heavy grey moustache'.[16] He had by then, it seems, overcome his gambling problems and said that he was determined to devote the rest of his life to 'rescuing men from the folly of gambling'.[17]

Even after the deaths of George and Austin, the legacy of crime in the Bidwell family continued. In March 1908 another of the Bidwell brothers, Benson Bidwell, age seventy-three, and his son, Charles F. Bidwell, were found guilty of 'operating a confidence game'.[18] Benson claimed to have invented 'an electric motor that would not burn out' and using his Bidwell Electric Co. placed advertisements looking for investment. Ironically, Austin had written to William Pinkerton in February 1898 asking him to invest:

> Dear Sir,
> I think you have been more or less cognisant of my brother Benson's Electrical Inventions. His success as an inventor has been great, but he has been unfortunate in the management of

his inventions. After many years, by our joint efforts, we have at length got our business in shape and have organized a Company with our headquarters in this city.

I enclose you some papers, which I think you may find interesting. You will see by them what we have and what we are trying to do, and we would be greatly pleased if you would take a few shares of our Stock, and while helping us out, make a good investment for yourself.

Very Respectfully,

Austin B. Bidwell.[19]

William Pinkerton replied to Austin, on behalf of his brother and himself, politely declining the offer:

... neither Mr Robt. A. Pinkerton or myself are in position to buy stock of any kind at the present time. We have notes to meet on property that we own and that will take all the spare money we can get together without taking any other property.

Your inventions look like a good thing and I hope it will be a success.[20]

The Pinkertons may not have been interested, but Benson and Charles did receive thousands of dollars in investment from other people. Ultimately, however, they were found to have deceived their investors. An employee of theirs even testified that at one exhibition their machine, some kind of perpetual motion device, began to overheat and emit smoke: 'Charles Bidwell sat near the exhibit blowing cigar smoke about it so that spectators might not discover the real cause of the fumes.'[21] The father and son were sentenced to 'a term of from one to ten years in the penitentiary'.[22] The elder Bidwell was defiant about his innocence:

I say honestly that I have never stolen a dollar or one cent of the Bidwell Electric Company's money. They charged me the same thing in Philadelphia when I invented the trolley car, but now it is running in every city in the world. I invented the electric fan, but, being too poor to take out a patent, I was deprived of the fruits of my work. The cold motor will develop just as well, and it will be used throughout the world after I am under the sod and forgotten.[23]

In the end a deal was done by which the father, whose health was failing in prison, was released in April 1909 in return for the son agreeing not to appeal and finishing out his sentence.[24]

Exactly how much of the money stolen from the Bank of England back in 1873 was never recovered is hard to establish. The police, and many in the press, estimated that the outstanding amount could be at least £60,000, and many people believed that the true figure was even higher than that.[25] Although they always denied it, rumours persisted to the end of their lives that George, Austin, Mac and Noyes were still in possession of a considerable amount of the money from the Great Fraud on the Bank of England. However, the lives led by the four perpetrators following their release from prison does not bear this rumour out. There is no evidence or sign of them having a large stash of money hidden away somewhere. George and Austin were forced to flog their stories around the country and overseas, in the form of books and lecture tours, while Mac and Noyes reverted back to criminality in order to survive. The truth is that never again were any of them able to replicate the opulent lifestyles that they had enjoyed in London in the early 1870s. But one must consider where that life of crime ultimately led them. As George himself said:

... the thirst for riches, once implanted, will lead any man to unthought-of depths of infamy.[26]

Notes

———•◦•———

Where I have quoted directly from contemporary sources, in the interest of simplicity and clarity and where it does not alter the meaning, on occasion I have altered the spelling, capitalization and punctuation.

Abbreviations used in Notes:

Bid., *Travels*: Bidwell, A., *Bidwell's Travels, from Wall Street to London Prison* (Hartford: Bidwell Publishing Company, 1897)

G. Bid., *Chains*: Bidwell, G., *Forging His Chains, The Autobiography of George Bidwell* (Hartford: SS. Scranton and Co., 1888)

G. Bid., *True History*: Bidwell, G., *True History of the So-Called £1,000,000 Forgery* (Hartford: Bidwell Publishing Company, 1891)

Kingston: Kingston, C., *Dramatic Days at the Old Bailey* (London: Stanley Paul & Co. Ltd, 1923)

Old Bailey: Old Bailey Proceedings Online (www.oldbaileyonline. org), August 1873, Trial of Austin Biron Bidwell, George Macdonnell, George Bidwell, Edwin Noyes Hills (t18730818-483)

Times: *The Times* newspaper, London

Pinkerton Files: Pinkerton's National Detective Agency Files, Part B: Criminal Case Files, available as a microfilm from LexisNexis (UPA) Collections, Pinkerton's National Detective Agency Files, Part B: Criminal Case File. Series 1: A-C, Reel 2

A. Pinkerton, *Thirty Years*: Pinkerton, A., *Thirty Years a Detective: A Thorough and Comprehensive Exposé of Criminal Practices of all Grades and Classes* (New York: G.W. Dillingham, 1900)

CHAPTER ONE

1 *The Times*, 31 May 1873, Mansion House, evidence of Mr Green.
2 Old Bailey, evidence of Mr Green.
3 Old Bailey, evidence of Mr Fenwick.
4 Old Bailey, evidence of Mr Fenwick; *The Times*, 31 May 1873.
5 *The Times*, 31 May 1873, Mansion House, evidence of Mr Fenwick.
6 Ibid.
7 *The Times*, 6 June 1873.
8 *The Times*, 31 May 1873, Mansion House, evidence of Col Francis.
9 *The Times*, 31 May 1873, Mansion House, evidence of Col Francis.
10 Cost as given in *The Times*, 4 March 1873.
11 Letter dated 28 December 1872; *The Times*, 31 May 1872, Mansion House, evidence of Col Francis; Old Bailey, evidence of Col Francis; *The Times*, 20 August 1873.

CHAPTER TWO

1 *The Times*, 22 August 1873, evidence of Mr Stanton.
2 *The Times*, 19 August 1873, Mr Giffard opening the case.
3 Old Bailey, evidence of James Richardson.
4 Old Bailey, evidence of James Richardson.
5 *The Times*, 22 August 1873, evidence of Mr Stanton.
6 *The Times*, 31 May 1873, Mansion House, evidence of Mr Fenwick and also evidence of Col Francis; Trial, Mr Fenwick's evidence; G. Bid., *Chains*, p.300; Old Bailey, evidence of Mr Fenwick.
7 *The Times*, 6 June 1873, Mansion House.
8 *The Times*, 31 May 1873, Mansion House, evidence of Col Francis.
9 Ibid.
10 Old Bailey, evidence of Col Francis.
11 G. Bid., *Chains*, p.203.
12 *The Times*, 20 August 1873.
13 Ibid.

CHAPTER THREE

1 *The Times*, 8 March 1873, evidence of Col Francis at Mansion House.
2 According to Col Francis at the Mansion House, *The Times*, 8 March 1873.
3 *The Times*, 8 March 1873, evidence of William Henry Trumpler at Mansion House; *The Times*, 15 March 1873.
4 G. Bid., *Chains*, p.300.

CHAPTER FOUR

1 *Dawson Daily News*, 7 September 1908, taken from *Lloyd's Weekly*, 8 August 1908.
2 Old Bailey, evidence of Pope.

3 *The Times*, 8 March 1873, evidence of Pope.
4 Old Bailey, evidence of Spittle; *The Times*, 8 March 1873, evidence of Spittle at Mansion House; *The Times*, 19 August 1873, Trial, Mr Giffard opening the case.
5 *The Times*, 3 March 1873.
6 Ibid.
7 Ibid.
8 Ibid.

CHAPTER FIVE

1 *Dawson Daily News*, 7 September 1908, from *Lloyd's Weekly*, 8 August 1908.
2 *The Times*, 8 March 1873.
3 *The Times*, 4 March 1873.
4 Ibid.
5 Ibid.
6 Ibid.
7 Ibid.
8 Ibid.
9 Ibid.

CHAPTER SIX

1 *The Times*, 8 March 1873; G. Bid., *Chains*, p.215.
2 *The Times*, 8 March 1873; G. Bid., *Chains*, p.216.
3 *The Times*, 8 March 1873.
4 Ibid.
5 Ibid.
6 *The Times*, 8 March 1873, evidence of Mr May.
7 *The Times*, 8 March 1873, evidence of Mr Flower.
8 *The Times*, 8 March 1873.
9 Ibid.
10 Ibid.
11 *The Times*, 8 March 1873, evidence of Spittle.
12 *The Times*, 8 March 1873.
13 Ibid.
14 *The Times*, 10 March and 12 March 1873; Pinkerton files.
15 *The Times*, 10 and 12 March 1873.
16 *The Times*, 10 March 1873.
17 *Illustrated London News*, Saturday 15 March 1873.

CHAPTER SEVEN

1 G. Bid., *Chains*, p.26.
2 G. Bid., *Chains*, p.24.
3 G. Bid., *Chains*, p.29.
4 G. Bid., *Chains*, p.29.

5 G. Bid., *Chains*, p.30.
6 G. Bid., *Chains*, p.31.
7 G. Bid., *Chains*, p.32.
8 Ibid.
9 Ibid.
10 G. Bid., *Chains*, p.33.
11 G. Bid., *Chains*, pp.35, 36.
12 G. Bid., *Chains*, pp.36, 37.
13 G. Bid., *Chains*, p.59.
14 G. Bid., *Chains*, pp.74, 75.
15 *The New York Times*, 9 March 1899.
16 Date of birth based on 1881 Census of England, thirty-five years of age at time.
17 A. Bid., *Travels*, p.24.
18 A. Bid., *Travels*, p.26.
19 Ibid.
20 G. Bid., *Chains*, p.134.
21 A. Bid., *Travels*, p.20.
22 G. Bid., *Chains*, p.135.
23 A. Bid., *Travels*, p.47.
24 *The New York Times*, 9 March 1899.
25 This was especially the case during the time when he was lobbying for Austin's release from prison in England.
26 A. Pinkerton, *Thirty Years*, p.418.
27 *The Times*, 7 March 1873.
28 *The Times*, 23 April 1873.
29 A. Bid., *Travels*, p.115.

CHAPTER EIGHT

1 G. Bid., *Chains*, p.132.
2 According to G. Bid., *Chains*, p.132; Some other accounts say that he was born in Canada and raised in the United States.
3 *Dawson Daily News*, 7 September 1908, quoting from *Lloyd's Weekly*, 8 August 1908.
4 A. Bid., *Travels*, p.132.
5 *The New York Times*, 2 April 1873.
6 G. Bid., *Chains*, p.137.
7 *The Times*, 11 April 1873, quoting from *The New York Times*.
8 *The Times*, 28 August 1873.
9 Details from A. Pinkerton, *Thirty Years*, pp.419–422.
10 A. Pinkerton, *Thirty Years*, p.420.
11 Ibid.
12 A. Pinkerton, *Thirty Years*, p.421.
13 A. Pinkerton, *Thirty Years*, p.421, 422.
14 *The New York Times*, 2 April 1873; *The Times*, 15 April 1873, quoting from *The Boston Advertiser*.

15 *The Times*, 15 April 1873, quoting from *The Boston Advertiser*.
16 This is surely our Noyes from the Great Fraud on the Bank of England.
17 *The Times*, 7 April 1873.
18 *The Times*, 7 April 1873; *The Times*, 11 April 1873, quoting from *The New York Times*.
19 *The Times*, 11 April 1873, quoting from *The New York Times*.
20 Ibid.
21 Ibid.
22 G. Bid., *Chains*, p.133.
23 *The New York Times*, 24 March 1876.
24 G. Bid., *Chains*, p.126.
25 G. Bid., *Chains*, p.125.
26 *The Times*, 15 April 1873, quoting from *The Boston Advertiser*.
27 *The New York Times*, 24 March 1876.
28 Ibid.
29 Ibid.

CHAPTER NINE

1 *The Times*, 11 April 1873, Mansion House.
2 Ibid.
3 G. Bid., *Chains*, p.188.
4 A. Bid., *Travels*, p.146.
5 Ibid.
6 A. Bid., *Travels*, p.149.
7 Old Bailey, evidence of E.H. Green.
8 A. Bid., *Travels*, p.200.
9 G. Bid., *Chains*, p.126.
10 G. Bid., *Chains*, p.152.
11 Old Bailey, Mac's statement; Old Bailey, evidence of Samuel Wilson Robinson.
12 G. Bid., *Chains*, p.174.
13 *The Times*, 26 April 1873.
14 Ibid.
15 *The Times*, 23 May 1873, Mansion House, evidence of Kate Mary English.
16 Ibid.
17 Ibid.
18 Ibid.
19 *The Times*, 19 August 1873, Trial, Mr Giffard opening the case; *The Times*, 27 August 1873.
20 G. Bid., *Chains*, p.185.
21 G. Bid., *Chains*, p.187.

CHAPTER TEN

1 G. Bid., *Chains*, p.190.
2 *The Times*, 15 March 1873.

3 Ibid.

4 Ibid.

5 *The Times*, 23 May 1873, Mansion House, evidence of Kate Mary English.

6 Ibid.

7 Old Bailey, evidence of Charles Chabot, handwriting expert.

8 *Dawson Daily News*, 7 September 1908, quoting from *Lloyd's Weekly*, 8 August 1908.

9 Ibid.

10 *The New York Times*, 2 April 1873; *The Times*, 15 April 1873, quoting from *The Boston Advertiser*; *The Times*, 28 August 1873, says he was sentenced to seven years in January 1869 but 'on the urgent appeals of his friends and relations a pardon was granted to him in March, 1872'.

11 *The Times*, 23 May 1873, Mansion House, evidence of Mr William Guest Barrett, purser.

12 Ibid.

13 *The Times*, 23 May 1873.

14 *The Times*, 23 May 1873, Mansion House, evidence of Mr William Guest Barrett, purser.

15 23 May 1873, Mansion House, evidence of Kate Mary English.

16 *Dawson Daily News*, 7 September 1908, quoting from *Lloyd's Weekly*, 8 August 1908.

17 *The Times*, 6 June 1873, Mansion House, evidence of Hagger.

18 *The Times*, 19 August 1873, Trial, Mr Giffard opening the case.

19 *The Times*, 8 March 1873, Mansion House.

20 G. Bid., *Chains*, p.195.

21 *The Times*, 15 March 1873.

22 *The Times*, 28 June 1873, Mansion House, entry in Noyes' diary seized by police and mentioned in Sergeant Spittle's evidence.

CHAPTER ELEVEN

1 *The Times*, 19 June 1873, Mansion House.

2 Ibid.

3 Ibid.

4 *The Times*, 19 August 1873, Trial, Mr Giffard opening the case.

5 G. Bid., *Chains*, p.193.

6 *The Times*, 14 June 1873, Mansion House, evidence of Lyell.

7 Ibid.

8 *The Times*, 14 June 1873, Mansion House, evidence of James Mowatt.

9 Ibid.

10 *The Times*, 3 May 1873, Mansion House, evidence of George Boole Challoner.

11 *The Times*, 3 May 1873.

12 Ibid.

13 Ibid.

14 *The Times*, 12 May 1873, Mansion House, evidence of Thomas Straker.

15 Ibid.

16 Ibid.

17 Ibid.
18 *The Times*, 12 May 1873, Mansion House, evidence of James Dalton.
19 *The Times*, 17 May 1873.
20 *The Times*, 17 May 1873, Mansion House, evidence of James Dalton.
21 *The Times*, 28 June 1873, Mansion House, evidence of Cheshire.
22 Ibid.

CHAPTER TWELVE

 1 A. Bid., *Travels*, pp.91, 92.
 2 *The Times*, 14 June 1873, Mansion House, evidence of Frances Grey (i.e. Daisy).
 3 *The Times*, 14 June 1873.
 4 Ibid.
 5 A. Bid., *Travels*, p.208.
 6 Old Bailey, Mac's statement.
 7 *The Times*, 21 August 1873, Trial, evidence of de Lorelli.
 8 A. Bid., *Travels*, p.211.
 9 *The Times*, 21 August 1873, Trial, evidence of de Lorelli and Heinreich.
10 *The Times*, 14 June 1873, Mansion House.
11 Old Bailey, Mac's statement.
12 Ibid.
13 *The Times*, 14 June 1873, Mansion House.

CHAPTER THIRTEEN

 1 G. Bid., *Chains*, p.199.
 2 G. Bid., *Chains*, p.201.
 3 G. Bid., *Chains*, p.204.
 4 *The Times*, 23 May 1873.
 5 Ibid.
 6 Ibid.
 7 *The Times*, 3 May 1873.
 8 Ibid.
 9 *The Times*, 21 March 1873.
10 Ibid.
11 Ibid.
12 *The Times*, 3 May 1873; Old Bailey, evidence of Lidington.
13 Old Bailey, evidence of Lidington.
14 *The Times*, 3 May 1873; Old Bailey, evidence of Lidington.
15 *The Times*, 21 March 1873.
16 Ibid.
17 *The Times*, 18 April 1873.
18 Ibid.
19 Ibid.
20 Ibid.
21 G. Bid., *Chains*, p.201.

22 G. Bid., *Chains*, p.205.
23 G. Bid., *Chains*, p.204.
24 Ibid.
25 G. Bid., *Chains*, p.205.

CHAPTER FOURTEEN

1 Old Bailey, evidence of James Noyes, Henry Thomas Hagger, William Mills, Thomas Henry Jessey.
2 *The Times*, 11 April 1873, Mansion House.
3 Ibid.
4 *The Times*, 6 June 1873, Mansion House, evidence of John Robert Gray.
5 G. Bid., *Chains*, p.205, 206.
6 Old Bailey; *The Times*, 27 August 1873.
7 *The Times*, 15 March 1873.
8 *The Times*, 17 May 1873, Mansion House, evidence of Joseph Meyer Bros.
9 Ibid.
10 *The Times*, 26 April 1873.
11 *The Times*, 26 April 1873, Mansion House, evidence of Wyatt.
12 *The Times*, 26 April 1873.
13 *The Times*, 18 April 1873.
14 *The Times*, 26 April 1873.
15 *The Times*, 18 April 1873, Mansion House, evidence of Nelly Vernon.
16 Ibid.
17 *The Times*, 15 March 1873.
18 Ibid.
19 *The Times*, 26 April 1873.
20 *The Times*, 15 March 1873.
21 Ibid.
22 Ibid.
23 *The Times*, 11 April 1873, Mansion House.
24 Old Bailey, evidence of Nelly Vernon; *The Times*, 18 April 1873, evidence of Nelly Vernon.

CHAPTER FIFTEEN

1 *Dawson Daily News*, 7 September 1908, taken from *Lloyd's Weekly*, 8 August 1908.
2 *The Times*, 11 April 1873, Mansion House.
3 *The Times*, 25 August 1873, Old Bailey Trial, the details read out in court by Mr Read, the Deputy Clerk of Arraigns.
4 *The Times*, 11 April 1873, Mansion House, Mr Poland.
5 *The Times*, 25 August 1873; *Times*, 11 April 1873, Mansion House, Mr Poland.
6 *The Times*, 25 August 1873, Trial, evidence of Franz Hérold.
7 Ibid.

CHAPTER SIXTEEN

1 *The Times*, 26 April 1873, Mansion House, evidence of Alexander Naylor.
2 *The Times*, 26 April 1873.
3 *The Times*, 26 April 1873, Mansion House, evidence of Alexander Naylor.
4 Ibid.
5 Ibid.
6 *The Times*, 6 June 1873, Mansion House, evidence of Alfred H. Reman, Manager.
7 Ibid.
8 *The Times*, 6 June 1873, Mansion House, evidence of Willard Brigham Farwell, the General Superintendent of the North Atlantic Express Company, New York.
9 *The Times*, 28 June 1873, Mansion House, evidence of Williams.
10 *The Times*, 6 June 1873, Mansion House, evidence of Willard Brigham Farwell.
11 *The New York Times*, 22 April 1873; *The Times*, 6 June 1873, Mansion House, evidence of Willard Brigham Farwell.
12 *The Times*, 6 June 1873, Mansion House, evidence of Willard Brigham Farwell.
13 *The New York Times*, 22 April 1873; *The Times*, 8 May 1873, 'From our American Correspondent, Philadelphia, April 22'.
14 *The Times*, 21 March 1872; *The Times*, 5 April 1873, Mansion House, evidence of James E. Smart.
15 Although later on payment was stopped by the courts; *The Times*, 5 April 1873; *The Times*, 21 March 1872.
16 *The Times*, 18 April 1873, Nelly Vernon's evidence at Mansion House; when Nelly was arrested she gave the ticket up to the police.
17 *The Times*, 23 May 1873, Mansion House, evidence of Kate Mary English.
18 *The Times*, 26 April 1873, Mansion House, evidence of William Mann.
19 *The Times*, 15 March 1873.
20 Ibid.
21 Ibid.
22 *The Times*, 18 April 1873, Nelly Vernon's evidence at Mansion House.
23 *The Times*, 15 March 1873.

CHAPTER SEVENTEEN

1 *The Times*, 15 March 1873.
2 Ibid.
3 Noyes would claim later that someone important from the bank did visit him with a bribe.
4 *The Times*, 15 March 1873.
5 Ibid.
6 Ibid.
7 Ibid.
8 *The Times*, 11 April 1873.

9   *The Times*, 15 March 1873.
10 Ibid.
11 Ibid.
12 *The Times*, 23 August 1873, Trial, evidence of Ellen Franklin.
13 Ibid.
14 *The Times*, 15 March 1873.
15 Ibid.
16 Ibid.
17 Ibid.
18 Ibid.
19 *The Times*, 23 August 1873, Trial, evidence of Helen Vernon.
20 *The Times*, 15 March 1873.
21 Ibid.
22 Ibid.
23 Ibid.
24 Ibid.
25 Ibid.
26 Ibid.
27 Ibid.
28 Ibid.
29 Ibid.
30 Ibid.
31 Ibid.
32 *The Times*, 26 April 1873; *The Times*, 11 April 1873, Mansion House, Mr Poland.

CHAPTER EIGHTEEN

1   *The Times*, 21 March 1873.
2   Ibid.
3   Old Bailey, evidence of Henry William Hughes.
4   *The Times*, 21 March 1873.
5   Ibid.
6   Ibid.
7   Ibid.
8   Ibid.
9   Ibid.
10 Ibid.
11 Ibid.
12 Ibid.
13 Ibid.

CHAPTER NINETEEN

1   A. Bid., *Travels*, p.276.
2   G. Bid., *Chains*, p.200.
3   Ibid.

4 A. Bid., *Travels*, p.276.
5 A. Bid., *Travels*, p.278.
6 A. Bid., *Travels*, pp.276.
7 A. Bid., *Travels*, p.277.
8 A. Bid., *Travels*, pp.282, 283.
9 A. Bid., *Travels*, pp.301, 302.
10 A. Bid., *Travels*, p.310.
11 A. Bid., *Travels*, p.313.
12 A. Bid., *Travels*, pp.314, 315.
13 A. Bid., *Travels*, p.316.
14 A. Bid., *Travels*, p.327, 328.
15 A. Bid., *Travels*, p.312.
16 A. Bid., *Travels*, p.332.
17 Ibid.
18 Ibid.
19 A. Bid., *Travels*, p.333.
20 A. Bid., *Travels*, p.334.
21 This story of an attempted escape and shooting is Austin's version of what happened that day as told in his book. It does not seem to be mentioned by anyone else who was there that day and would make one wonder why, if he had really attempted to shoot someone, so many people would have been convinced of his innocence at the beginning. One suspects that it may have been an attempt by him to inject some extra drama into his story.
22 *New York Herald*, Editorial, 26 February 1873.
23 A. Bid., *Travels*, p.338.
24 A. Bid., *Travels*, p.345.
25 *The New York Times*, 13 April 1873.
26 *The Times*, 14 April 1873.
27 A. Bid., *Travels*, p.345.
28 A. Bid., *Travels*, p.347.
29 A. Bid., *Travels*, p.348.
30 A. Bid., *Travels*, pp.348, 349.
31 A. Bid., *Travels*, p.358.
32 A. Bid., *Travels*, p.368.
33 A. Bid., *Travels*, pp.370, 371.
34 *The Times*, 5 April 1873.
35 Ibid.
36 *The Times*, 11 April 1873.
37 *The Times*, 6 May 1873, 'From Our American Correspondent, Philadelphia, April 15'.
38 *The Times* quoted in A. Bid., *Travels*, pp.374, 375.
39 Old Bailey, evidence of Hayden; according to Hayden, these were given over to them on 8 May by Vice-Consul Mr Crawford.
40 Old Bailey, evidence of Hayden.

CHAPTER TWENTY

1 *The Times*, 14 June 1873, Mansion House.
2 Ibid.
3 Old Bailey, Evidence of Catherine Grey; *The Times*, 14 June 1873, Mansion House.
4 *The Times*, 11 April 1873, Mansion House.
5 *The Times*, 7 April 1873.
6 *The Times*, 19 June 1873, Mansion House.
7 *The Times*, 3 April 1873, 'From Our American Correspondent, Philadelphia, March 21'.
8 *The Times*, 3 April 1873.
9 *The New York Times*, 8 May 1873.
10 *The Times*, 3 April 1873.
11 Ibid.
12 Ibid.
13 *The Times*, 21 March 1873.
14 *The Times*, 11 April 1873, quoting *The New York Times*.
15 *The New York Times*, 5 April 1873.
16 *The Times*, 7 April 1873.
17 Ibid.
18 *The New York Times*, 25 April 1873.
19 *The New York Times*, 8 May 1873.
20 *The Times*, 27 May 1873, 'From Our American Correspondent, Philadelphia, May 9'.
21 *The New York Times*, 4 June 1873.
22 *The Times*, 19 June 1873, Mansion House.
23 *The New York Times*, 5 June 1873.
24 Ibid.

CHAPTER TWENTY-ONE

1 *The Times*, 11 April 1873, Mr Poland at the Mansion House.
2 *The Times*, 5 April 1873, Mansion House, evidence of Smith.
3 Ibid.
4 G. Bid., *Chains*, p.220.
5 Ibid.
6 G. Bid., *Chains*, p.221.
7 A. Bid., *Travels*, p.249.
8 Ibid.
9 *The Times*, 11 April 1873; *The Times*, 18 April 1873.
10 *The New York Times*, 2 April 1873.
11 G. Bid., *Chains*, p.226.
12 G. Bid., *Chains*, p.227.
13 G. Bid., *Chains*, p.228.
14 G. Bid., *Chains*, p.234.
15 G. Bid., *Chains*, p.235.

16 A. Bid., *Travels*, p.266; G. Bid., *Chains*, p.237, 'By cable to *New York Herald*, London, March 18, 1873'.
17 *The Times*, 18 March 1873.
18 G. Bid., *Chains*, p.238.
19 *The Times*, 11 April 1873.
20 Old Bailey; *The Times*, 27 August 1873; *The Times*, 11 April 1873.
21 Old Bailey; *The Times*, 19 August 1873, Trial, Mr Giffard opening the case; *The Times*, 27 August 1873.
22 Old Bailey; *The Times*, 27 August 1873.
23 Ibid.
24 Addressed to Mr Alfred J. Watson, Brevoort House, Fifth Avenue, New York.
25 Old Bailey, evidence of Ann Thomas; *Times*, 11 April 1873.
26 That seal was later found in George Bidwell's possession.
27 *The Times*, 18 April 1873.
28 Ibid.
29 Ibid.
30 Ibid.
31 Ibid.

CHAPTER TWENTY-TWO

1 *The Times*, 4 April 1873.
2 *The Times*, 5 April 1873, Mansion House, evidence of McKelvie.
3 Ibid.
4 Ibid.
5 Ibid.
6 Ibid.
7 *The Times*, 4 April 1873.
8 *The Times*, 5 April 1873.
9 *The Times*, 18 April 1873.
10 Ibid.
11 *The Times*, 4 April 1873.
12 *The Times*, 11 April 1873.
13 *The Times*, 4 April 1873.
14 *The Times*, 5 April 1873.
15 *The Times*, 4 April 1873.
16 *The Times*, 5 April 1873, Spittle in answer to Dr Kenealy and Mr Lewis at the Mansion House.
17 *The Times*, 5 April 1873, Mansion House, evidence of Smith and Spittle.
18 Old Bailey, Spittle.
19 *The Times*, 5 April 1873, Mansion House, evidence of Smith.
20 *The Times*, 4 April 1873.
21 *The Times*, 5 April 1873, Mansion House, evidence of Spittle.
22 *The Times*, 5 April 1873, Mansion House, evidence of Smith.
23 *The Times*, 4 April 1873.
24 *The Times*, 5 April 1873, Mansion House, evidence of Spittle.

25 *The Times*, 5 April 1873, Mansion House, evidence of Spittle; Old Bailey, evidence of Spittle.
26 *The Times*, 4 April 1873.

CHAPTER TWENTY-THREE

 1 *The Times*, 5 April 1873.
 2 Ibid.
 3 Ibid.
 4 Ibid.
 5 Ibid.
 6 Ibid.
 7 Ibid.
 8 Ibid.
 9 Ibid.
10 Ibid.
11 Ibid.
12 Ibid.
13 G. Bid., *Chains*, p.262.
14 G. Bid., *Chains*, p.263.
15 *The Times*, 11 April 1873.
16 G. Bid., *Chains*, p.265.
17 *The Times*, 18 April 1873.
18 Ibid.
19 Ibid.
20 Ibid.
21 Ibid.
22 Ibid.
23 Ibid.
24 Ibid.
25 Ibid.
26 Ibid.
27 *The Times*, 26 April 1873.
28 *The Times*, 26 April 1873; *Times*, 23 May 1873.

CHAPTER TWENTY-FOUR

 1 A. Bid., *Travels*, p.379.
 2 *Times*, 29 May 1873.
 3 Ibid.
 4 Ibid.
 5 Ibid.
 6 Ibid.
 7 Ibid.
 8 *The Times*, 31 May 1873.
 9 Ibid.
10 *The Times*, 6 June 1873.

11 *The Times*, 18 June 1873; *The Times*, 19 June 1873.
12 *The Times*, 18 June 1873.

CHAPTER TWENTY-FIVE

 1 A. Bid., *Travels*, p.380.
 2 *The Times*, 19 June 1873, Mansion House.
 3 Ibid.
 4 *The Times*, 1 July 1873, Mansion House.
 5 *The Times*, 13 August 1873.
 6 *The Times*, 1 July 1873, Mansion House.
 7 Ibid.
 8 Ibid.
 9 *The Times*, 3 July 1873, Mansion House.
10 Ibid.
11 Ibid.
12 Ibid.
13 *The Times*, 13 August 1873.
14 Ibid.
15 Ibid.
16 G. Bid., *Chains*, p.276.
17 *The Times*, 3 July 1873, Mansion House.
18 Ibid.
19 Ibid.
20 Ibid.
21 *The Times*, 13 August 1873.
22 *The Times*, 28 June 1873.
23 *The Times*, 28 June 1873, Vice-Chancellors' Courts.
24 Ibid.
25 Ibid.
26 *The Times*, 4 July 1873.
27 *The Times*, 18 July 1873.
28 G. Bid., *Chains*, p.272.
29 G. Bid., *Chains*, p.273.
30 G. Bid., *Chains*, p.274.
31 G. Bid., *Chains*, p.273.
32 G. Bid., *Chains*, p.275.

CHAPTER TWENTY-SIX

 1 *The Times*, 8 July 1873.
 2 Ibid.
 3 G. Bid., *Chains*, pp.276, 277.
 4 *The Times*, 9 July 1873.
 5 Ibid.
 6 Ibid.
 7 Ibid.

8 Ibid.
9 Ibid.
10 Ibid.

CHAPTER TWENTY-SEVEN

1 G. Bid., *Chains*, p.365.
2 *The Times*, 19 August 1873.
3 Ibid.
4 Ibid.
5 Ibid.
6 Ibid.
7 *The Times*, 13 August 1873.
8 *The Times*, 27 August 1873.
9 Ibid.
10 Ibid.
11 Ibid.
12 Ibid.
13 Ibid.
14 G. Bid., *Chains*, p.381.
15 *The Times*, 27 August 1873.
16 Ibid.
17 *The Times*, 27 August 1873; G. Bid., *Chains*, p.381.
18 *The Times*, 27 August 1873.
19 Ibid.
20 Ibid.
21 Ibid.
22 Ibid.
23 Ibid.
24 G. Bid., *Chains*, pp.381–3.
25 *The Times*, 27 August 1873.
26 Ibid.
27 *The Times*, 27 August 1873; G. Bid., *Chains*, p.383.
28 G. Bid., *Chains*, p.399.
29 A. Bid., *Travels*, p.386.
30 A. Bid., *Travels*, p.389.

CHAPTER TWENTY-EIGHT

1 *The Times*, 27 August 1873.
2 Kingston, p.81.
3 *Illustrated London News*, 20 September 1873.
4 Pinkerton Files.
5 Pinkerton Files.
6 *Illustrated London News*, 30 August 1873.
7 Ibid.
8 Ibid.

9 G. Bid., *Chains*, p.400.
10 G. Bid., *Chains*, p.45.
11 G. Bid., *Chains*, note p.383.
12 A. Bid., *Travels*, p.383.
13 A. Bid., *Travels*, p.388.
14 Ibid.
15 G. Bid., *Chains*, p.398.
16 G. Bid., *Chains*, p.265.
17 G. Bid., *Chains*, p.266.
18 G. Bid., *Chains*, pp.266, 267.
19 A. Bid., *Travels*, p.384.
20 Ibid.
21 A. Bid., *Travels*, p.478.
22 *The Times*, 25 August 1873; G. Bid., *Chains*, p.385.
23 *The Times*, 25 August 1873.
24 G. Bid., *Chains*, p.387 quoting from *The Times*, 25 August 1873.
25 *The Times*, 25 August 1873.
26 G. Bid., *Chains*, p.388.
27 G. Bid., *Chains*, p.387.
28 G. Bid., *Chains*, p.268.
29 G. Bid., *Chains*, p.387.
30 G. Bid., *True History*, note p.197.
31 *The Times*, 16 October 1873.
32 Ibid.
33 Ibid.
34 Ibid.
35 Ibid.
36 *The Times*, 23 October 1873.
37 Ibid.
38 Ibid.
39 Ibid.
40 *The Times*, 26 November 1873; *Illustrated London News*, 29 November 1873.
41 A. Bid., *Travels*, p.375.
42 *The Times*, 13 October 1874, ' From our American Correspondent, Philadelphia, September 28'.
43 Ibid.

CHAPTER TWENTY-NINE

1 G. Bid., *Chains*, p.17.
2 G. Bid., *Chains*, p.18.
3 A. Bid., *Travels*, p.393.
4 A. Bid., *Travels*, p.187.
5 A. Bid., *Travels*, p.398.
6 *The New York Times*, 20 August 1892.
7 G. Bid., *Chains*, p.18.
8 G. Bid., *Chains*, p.456.

9 *The New York Times*, 20 August 1892.
10 Ibid.
11 G. Bid., *Chains*, p.19.
12 G. Bid., *Chains*, p.18.
13 G. Bid., *Chains*, p.19.
14 *The New York Times*, 4 August 1887.
15 Ibid.
16 G. Bid., *Chains*, pp.21, 22.
17 G. Bid., *Chains*, p.22.
18 *The New York Times*, 4 August 1887.
19 Ibid.
20 G. Bid., *Chains*, p.394.
21 G. Bid., *Chains*, p.396.
22 *The New York Times*, 20 August 1892.
23 Pinkerton Files, *The Evening News*, Chicago, 8 March 1892.
24 G. Bid., *True History*, note, p.197.
25 *The New York Times*, 27 September 1891; *The New York Times*,
    2 September 1891 quoting the *Pall Mall Gazette*; *The New York Times*,
    20 August 1892.
26 *The New York Times*, 20 August 1892.
27 A. Bid., *Travels*, p.480.
28 *The New York Times*, 20 August 1892.
29 Ibid.
30 *The New York Times*, 22 February 1892.
31 *The New York Times*, 28 February 1893.

CHAPTER THIRTY

1 *The New York Times*, 26 February 1892.
2 *The New York Times*, 9 March 1899; *The New York Times*, 27 March
   1899.
3 *The New York Times*, 9 March 1899.
4 Ibid.
5 *The New York Times*, 27 March 1899.
6 Ibid.
7 *Boston Evening Transcript*, 27 March 1899.
8 *The New York Times*, 28 February 1893.
9 Ibid.
10 Ibid.
11 Ibid.
12 *The New York Times*, 23 January 1897.
13 Ibid.
14 *Duluth Evening Herald*, 29 May 1905.
15 *Dawson Daily News*, 7 September 1908, quoting from *Lloyd's Weekly*, 8
    August 1908.
16 *Otago Witness*, 2 September 1908.
17 Ibid.

18 *The New York Times*, 15 March 1908.
19 Pinkerton Files.
20 Ibid.
21 *The New York Times*, 15 March 1908.
22 *The New York Times*, 25 October 1908.
23 Ibid.
24 *The New York Times*, 25 April 1909.
25 *The New York Times*, 20 August 1892.
26 G. Bid., *Chains*, p.146